Urban Magic & Mysticism

A Practical Guide to Discreet Rituals, Grounding in Small Spaces and Fitting Sacred Practices into a Busy Schedule to Integrate Spirituality into Your Daily Life

George Munson

Contents

Introduction

Have you ever felt that an ordinary moment suddenly becomes charged with meaning? A traffic light turns green as your favorite song starts. A crow lands in your path, watching you. You whisper a wish into your coffee steam, or think of someone just before they text. These moments stir the part of us that wants to believe life is more than what's visible. Yet for many, magic or mysticism feels just out of reach, reserved for ancient times or those with secret knowledge.

The search for modern magic often feels overwhelming and confusing. Countless sources give conflicting advice, making it easy to doubt whether you belong in this world or can do it 'right.' This book is here to simplify the process, offering clarity and reassurance for anyone seeking meaningful, practical magic in daily life.

I know what it feels like to crave something deeper and to get tangled up in confusion and doubt. Years ago, I found myself with a pile of books, a head full of questions, and a deep longing for connection, tradition, creativity, and something bigger than myself. I'm passionate about making magic and mysticism accessible, practical, and ethical for adults in the modern world. I want you to feel confident, supported, and creative, not constrained by confusing rules.

I will help you cut through the noise. You'll get clear rituals, practical frameworks, and a toolkit for building a practice that feels real, meaningful, and responsible. No more feeling like you don't belong or wondering if you're doing it wrong. This is about finding your way, with respect for tradition and space for your unique spark.

This book is for adults who are curious, creative, a bit skeptical, and looking to blend ancient wisdom with modern life. You might be new or want to go deeper. You could be an artist, a thinker, a caregiver, or anyone seeking more meaning in daily life. All you need is an open mind and a willingness to try.

What makes this book different is its foundation in history and genuine respect for diverse cultures. Unlike others, it is hands-on and practical, offering step-by-step rituals, ethical guidelines, creative exercises, and modular frameworks tailored for busy lives. Each chapter empowers you to experiment safely, personalize your experience, and progress at your pace.

I know some readers are skeptics. Maybe you doubt magic or dislike anything that sounds woo-woo. That's good. This book values questions and doubt. I won't ask you to take things on faith. You'll find space for curiosity, skepticism, and personal choice. Believers are welcome too. We're building a practice that invites uncertainty and discovery.

We'll begin with the roots, how magic and mysticism evolved, and what history teaches. Next, you'll get practical techniques and rituals, with clear steps and room for adaptation. We'll discuss ethics, cultural respect, and safe practice. You'll learn to interpret symbols and archetypes, and reflect on your personal meanings. Mindfulness exercises, journaling prompts, and creative challenges help deepen your practice. We'll cover art, music, community, and address what to do when things feel flat or lonely. Finally, we'll explore how to make magic a lasting part of your daily life.

You can build your own magical practice. You don't need permission or perfection. You can question, experiment, fail, and start again. This book supports your agency and curiosity. It helps you trust your instincts, celebrate creativity, and find what works for you.

By the time you reach the last page, you'll have more than knowledge. You'll have practical skills, ethical frameworks, and creative inspiration.

Most of all, you'll have the confidence and tools to make magic and mysticism an enriching part of your everyday life.

Take your first step now, and let's begin this journey together. Open the next page, your adventure starts here.

Chapter One

Foundations for the Modern Mystic

There's a comforting pause before you step out, keys in hand, when you set an intention, maybe for a smooth commute or a bit of patience. This isn't dramatic magic, just a daily ritual of focus. If you pay attention, the mystical can show up in these ordinary moments.

Many adults want something deeper but get lost in jargon, stereotypes, and debates about the "right" way to practice. Looking for guidance can feel like you have to pick sides or prove yourself. The truth is, magic and mysticism are related but different, and both have a place in modern life. Before you start rituals or meditation, take time to figure out what you really want. Knowing these fundamental differences can help clear up confusion from the start.

Unravel Key Distinctions for Today's Seeker of Magic vs. Mysticism

Let's start by defining the two terms. Magic is about using intention, rituals, symbols, or words to shift reality, either outside yourself or within. This could be as simple as lighting a candle for prosperity or making a sigil for courage. The word comes from the Greek "magos," which was associated with rituals intended to influence events. Aleister Crowley called magic "the Science and Art of causing Change to occur in conformity with Will." In the end, magic is about getting results, whether through small actions or big gestures.

Mysticism is about feeling connected to something greater, whether that's the Divine, the Universe, or a sense of Oneness. The word comes from the Greek "mystikos," meaning "secret" or "hidden." Instead of trying to change outside events, mysticism focuses on inner transformation or joining with something beyond yourself. Evelyn Underhill described mysticism as "the direct apprehension of the Divine," which is more about letting go than taking control. While magic asks, "How can I shape this moment?" mysticism asks, "How can I join with something larger?" The difference is in their goals: changing reality versus finding union.

These approaches lead to different experiences and questions. If you want more abundance, a magical approach might use a small ritual with coins, herbs, and affirmations to shift energy. A mystical approach would focus on meditating to connect with the abundance that's already there. Sometimes the lines blur; you might begin with a spell and end up meditating, or vice versa.

Forget the Hollywood version. Magic isn't just about rituals, old books, or wands. It often shows up in small ways, like setting an intention before bed, carrying a lucky stone, or quietly saying thanks over your coffee. Mystical experiences aren't always dramatic visions or ecstasy; they're often about quiet clarity or sitting calmly with your doubts. Pop culture makes things bigger than they are, but real experiences are usually more peaceful and more personal, ranging from subtle to profound.

You don't have to choose just one path. Most people mix both, often without noticing, maybe doing a spell and then journaling about dreams that feel like messages. Some days you'll want results, other days you'll want connection. Your practice can change as you do. As you think about it, notice how both paths might already be part of your daily life.

Where do you currently stand on these paths?

This check-in leads into practical self-examination.

Consider these prompts:

Are you more drawn to tangible results (manifesting, changing your mood/luck), or to direct feelings of unity and transcendence, or both?

What makes you feel spiritually fulfilled: visible change or deep internal connection?

Write down your thoughts. Notice which way you lean, and remember that this might change over time. Reflecting like this is a kind of magic; it helps you see what matters most to you right now.

To go further, think about the mindset you bring to these practices.

Balancing skepticism, curiosity, and self-trust gives you a strong foundation for your journey.

There's power in starting practice with a beginner's mind: open, curious, and humble. Wonder keeps learning fresh, no matter how much experience you have. Even experienced practitioners go back to simple acts and find new meaning. When you stop expecting things to stay the same, familiar rituals can reveal something new. Letting go makes room for growth. You encounter practices that promise big results or claim ancient roots. Actually, a healthy dose of critical thinking keeps your practice grounded. You don't need to believe everything simply because it sounds mystical or comes from a charismatic teacher. If you read advice that guarantees instant transformation or promises to fix your life overnight, pause and investigate. Ask yourself: Does this make sense? Does it align with your experience? It's wise to check sources, look for teachers who cite their sources, admit what they don't know, and invite questions rather than demand blind faith. If something feels off, it probably deserves another look. Skepticism isn't a barrier; it's a compass that helps you navigate hype and find what actually works for you.

Curiosity is your best guide. Think of your practice like a science experiment; it's less about being right or wrong and more about trying things and noticing what happens. Maybe you light a candle with gratitude, do your ritual or meditation, and then see how you feel. Not every experiment will be amazing; some might feel flat, while others bring small surprises. Playful, low-pressure rituals let you explore without stress. Try sitting quietly for five minutes and noticing your breath before and after, or write down an intention, fold it up, and keep it somewhere special for a week. These small experiments help you build confidence without needing everything to be perfect.

Self-trust grows when you value your own experience more than other people's rules. Your body, intuition, and gut feelings are good guides. If something feels right, pay attention. If a ritual makes you anxious or disconnected, trust that feeling too. Change or drop any practice that doesn't work for you. This is your path, and only you can decide where it goes.

Think of a time when your intuition guided you, maybe you avoided something that felt wrong or made a choice on a hunch that worked out. That's proof your inner compass is working. The more you listen to yourself, the easier it gets to tell real insight from outside noise.

Remembering Intuitive Wisdom

Spend five minutes remembering a time when you trusted your intuition, and it helped you, even in a small way. Maybe you took a different route home and saved time, reached out to a friend just when they needed it, or paused before sending an email and changed your words for clarity. Write down what happened: How did it feel in your body? What made you act? How did things turn out? Notice what this memory shows about the ability. When you balance skepticism, curiosity, and self-trust, you can learn at your own pace. This keeps magic and mysticism alive as real, changing practices instead of fixed systems. You don't need to be an expert or get rid of every doubt. Just stay open and honest. With time, this mindset makes every ritual a unique experience.

Building Your Personal Practice on a Firm Foundation

To create a practice that really fits your life, start by thinking of your rituals as building blocks you can mix and match. Instead of following someone else's script, use each part, like setting an intention, grounding, showing gratitude, or letting go of something, as a tool. You might light a candle, write down what you want to release, or sit and breathe. Use only the parts that feel right for you at the moment. You can shape your ritual to fit your mood, your time, or even the weather. The goal isn't to be perfect, but to make space for a genuine connection on your own terms.

Copying rituals from books or guides can help when you're learning, but if you repeat words or steps without meaning, your practice can become empty. Real change comes from being present with what you do. An actual practice means noticing how each step feels in your body and mind. Are you tense, relaxed, energized, or distracted? If you find yourself just going through the motions, pause and ask, "How does this feel right now?" Some parts might feel right, others might feel awkward. Use that feedback. Adjust as needed; you can change, skip, or swap out any part. Replacing chanting with your favorite song or leaving out a step isn't failure; it's growth.

Keeping track of your rituals helps you see what works best for you. A simple ritual journal can help. Write down the date, time, what you did, how you felt before and after, and any changes you noticed in the days that followed. Did you feel lighter or notice a mood shift? If not, that's important to note too. Over time, these notes become a map of your spiritual journey, showing what most supports you. You can also use quick checklists to rate your confidence, comfort, and connection. At first, lighting a candle or saying an intention out loud might feel awkward, but with practice, it becomes natural. Celebrate these changes; they show that consistency matters more than big gestures. Regular practice, even with quick "micro-practices," helps you build steady momentum. These don't have to be dramatic, just a few slow breaths before getting up, whispering an intention while making coffee, lighting a candle, or reflecting at dusk. Small acts like these keep you grounded in the present and show that meaningful ritual doesn't need fancy tools. The more you do these small things for yourself, the more grounded and confident you'll feel. The more grounded and confident you become.

Think of micro-practices like brushing your teeth or stretching, they're basic investments in your well-being. Not every ritual will feel magical. Some days will feel rushed or flat, others might bring unexpected clarity or comfort. What matters is showing up in ways that fit your actual life. Over time, simple acts create a solid foundation, a practice you can rely on through both good days and tough ones.

A Journal Template for Tracking Your Ritual Progress

Date/Time:
Ritual Components Used (intention, grounding, gratitude, release, etc.):
Mood/Body Sensations Before:
Mood/Body Sensations After:
Notable Events or Insights (same day/afterward):
Confidence Level (1–5):
Comfort Level (1–5):
What resonated?
What felt off?

Try this template for a week and watch for emerging patterns. You may be surprised at the growing clarity and confidence that comes from noticing small changes and honoring your process.

The foundation of your practice is flexibility paired with honest self-reflection. Give yourself permission to experiment and adapt as needed. Your rituals should evolve as you do; what works now may change over time. This process isn't about finding the perfect technique, but building an ongoing, real connection with yourself and the world through daily intention and care.

A Side-by-Side Guide to Major Traditions for Navigating the Maze

Exploring magical and mystical traditions can feel overwhelming, especially when you start with Wicca or Tarot and soon find yourself curious about Kabbalah or Taoist alchemy. The sheer range may leave you wondering whether you have to pick one path or if mixing practices is allowed. I've been there, moving from structured systems to poetic philosophies, searching for something practical and meaningful. Comparing major traditions side by side, with their main symbols, practices, and values, can make the landscape less daunting.

Here's a quick reference for easy comparison:

Tradition	Core Symbols	Typical Practices	Core Values
Wicca	Pentacle, elements	Sabbats, moon rituals, spells	Nature reverence, balance
Hermeticism	Caduceus, Tarot, alchemy	Meditation, correspondences	Unity of all things, wisdom
Kabbalah	Tree of Life	Pathworking, sacred study	Divine connection, insight
Taoist Alchemy	Yin-Yang, Bagua	Breathwork, inner alchemy	Harmony with Tao, longevity
Sufism	Heart, whirling dance	Chanting (dhikr), poetry	Divine love, surrender
Chaos Magic	Sigils, pop culture icons	Experimentation, belief-shifting	Pragmatism, flexibility

Each tradition offers distinct flavors and philosophies. Wicca is nature-focused, celebrating seasonal cycles and using ritual tools. Hermeticism weaves together science, magic, and philosophy, finding meaning in symbols like the Tarot and the caduceus. Kabbalah uses the Tree of Life for deep spiritual work. Taoist alchemy is inward-focused, emphasizing breathwork and energy practices to align with the Tao. Sufism uses poetry and movement for experiences of divine love. Chaos Magic is flexible and pragmatic, using any tool or system that works, even pop culture, with belief itself seen as a tool.

You'll notice some overlap. For instance, Tarot features in both Hermeticism and modern Kabbalah: one uses it for meditation and spiritual progress, while the other uses it as a guide on the Tree of Life. Both Taoist alchemy and Sufism incorporate breath and movement, but their end goals differ: cosmic harmony versus divine union.

Blending traditions and taking an eclectic approach is common today. Many personalize their practice, maybe by lighting candles like in Wicca, meditating on the Tree of Life (Kabbalah), and writing a Chaos Magic sigil before a big day. Often, people do this without claiming a particular label or title.

The benefit is flexibility and creativity: you shape your practice to meet your needs, free from rigid rules. You can experiment, adopting what resonates and letting go of what doesn't. There's no one auditing your choices. But there are risks: you might only skim the surface of a tradition, miss important context, or end up using practices in ways their originators would find careless or disrespectful.

For example, I met someone who paired Tarot (from Hermetic traditions) with mindfulness meditation (from Buddhist teaching), journaling their insights each day. They didn't claim a label; they followed honest curiosity and gained self-awareness that no single tradition had given them. Stories like these show the value in mindful mixing, but also the need for care.

If you're considering blending traditions, move thoughtfully. Here's a checklist to ensure your practice is thoughtful and respectful:

Is This Practice Appropriate?

- Do I know the origins of this practice?

- Am I using it respectfully, not just for aesthetics?

- Have I learned its cultural significance from authentic voices?

- Is it a closed practice (for initiates or community members only) or open?

- Do I credit the source if I share it?

- Am I willing to listen if someone from that tradition says, "Please don't?"

Seek out primary sources and practitioners for a deeper understanding, look for books, podcasts, or essays by those living the tradition. Community forums and good teachers can clarify both their expertise and limits, rooting your practice in genuine respect for traditions, not superficial trends.

Suggested resources:

- Visit local spiritual bookstores for meetups or author events.

- Search platforms like YouTube or practitioner podcasts.

- Explore library archives or museum websites for history and context.

Curiosity and respect go hand in hand: experiment, but stay aware of context and origins. Aim for a path that lets you be both creative and responsible.

Use Invisible Magic to Practice Discreetly in Modern Life

Magic doesn't need incense, bells, or salt circles; its power often lies in the quietest gestures, hidden in your daily routine. If you share spaces with others or want privacy around your spiritual practice, you're not alone. Many people have created meaningful routines in environments where candles can't be burned or in public places where privacy is rare. The key?

Invisible magic: practices that naturally blend into daily life, unnoticed by others.

Begin with the smallest, most discreet acts. Mentally repeat a silent mantra while on public transit to ground yourself without uttering a word. Carry a stone or coin in your pocket, feeling its weight for reassurance or courage. On busy mornings, devote a few seconds to infusing your coffee mug with intention by simply holding it and silently setting your energy for the day. These rituals, hidden in plain sight, are yours alone.

Privacy matters, especially in environments where discussing magic might attract gossip or unwanted attention. One example: someone hid her magical journal among work notebooks, using coded language and disguising gratitude lists as mundane to-dos. Everyday objects can become magical tools, a spoon stirring intention into soup, a scarf as an altar cloth, or a beloved ring as a talisman. Tuck small magical items into your bag, or use your phone's background as a "digital altar," a sacred image invisible to others.

For low-key altars, get creative. A drawer filled with meaningful mementos, pebbles, ribbons, and pressed flowers can serve as a secret, sacred space. A phone app folder with intention notes, loved ones' photos, or meditation playlists can serve the same purpose. There's no need for special supplies; magic adapts to your circumstances.

Fear of judgment is real, especially for those from communities wary of anything unconventional. Yet quiet acts like mindful dishwashing, treating it as a cleansing ritual, expressing gratitude, can be deeply empowering. Blessing your space by pausing before entering and inviting peace can look ordinary, but it can transform your inner world.

Seeing the mundane as magical shifts your mindset. Everyday acts, walking barefoot, tidying your space with intention, folding laundry, become rituals. The boundary between "ritual" and "routine" fades. Rather than seeking elaborate tools, notice what you already use that could be charged with meaning: a kitchen becomes a temple, a desk becomes an altar, a pen becomes a wand for affirmations.

Household items easily take on magical uses. A spoon embodies lunar energy and can stir up new beginnings; a mug holds moon water as well as a ceremonial chalice. A scarf draped on your lap offers a sacred space for reflection; brushing your teeth can be an opportunity for a whispered intention, and making your bed can become a moment for a silent blessing.

With time, these practices foster confidence and intimacy. Soon, you'll notice subtle shifts, a steadier mood after a mindful pause, a spark of inspiration from a lucky charm, comfort from knowing your magic is alive even when unseen. You don't need perfect conditions: your rituals fit any environment, quietly empowering you in the ordinary course of life.

There's no single right way to practice invisible magic. What's most important is that it suits your needs and circumstances. If you feel anxious about being discovered, remember: hidden magic is no less powerful. In fact, its privacy can make it even more meaningful, as it becomes intimately woven into your daily reality.

Ultimately, every moment can hold connection and purpose, no matter how routine it may appear. You carry the sacred with you, invisible yet present, always ready to offer comfort, clarity, and a reminder that magic belongs in modern life.

Chapter Two

Lineages, and Cultural Contexts

Tracing the Roots From Hermeticism to Folk Magic

Stories handed down over time, whispered charms to stop bleeding, and secret books hidden in attics show that magic and mysticism are not just things of the past. They are part of daily life, shaped by history, power, and our ongoing search for meaning. If you have ever wondered why a ritual feels mysterious, or why certain symbols show up in both movies and old church windows, you are connecting with a long, changing web of traditions.

Western magic as we know it began in Hellenistic Egypt. In cities like Alexandria during the early centuries CE, Greek, Egyptian, and Jewish thinkers came together. This mix led to Hermeticism, a system that combined Egyptian temple wisdom, Greek philosophy, and Jewish mysticism. The mythical figure Hermes Trismegistus stood for hidden knowledge and transformation. Hermetic texts taught about the unity of all things, the power of symbols and words, and the idea that people could reach the divine through secret knowledge (gnosis). These ideas spread beyond libraries and had a big impact on alchemy, astrology, and early science.

In medieval Europe, grimoires, manuals of magic, were shared among educated clergy and scholars. Ceremonial magic was complex, involving lengthy prayers in ancient languages, detailed diagrams, and specialized tools. Magicians who wrote books like the "Key of Solomon" believed that following strict rituals would let them command spirits or angels. Only the educated elite had access to these books, and they were often hidden to avoid persecution.

Magic was not only for scholars. In every village, wise people used charms, herbs, or spells to heal and protect others. These folk practices spread from rural England to West Africa and the Caribbean, wherever people needed hope. While ceremonial magicians performed complex rituals, practical knowledge was shared through stories, recipes, and experience. Enslaved people in Africa and the Americas mixed their traditions with Christianity, leading to practices like Hoodoo and Vodou.

Social forces had a big impact on these traditions. Rulers who wanted control often blamed magical practitioners, as seen in the witch hunts. Suppression did not erase these practices; it just pushed them underground. Some religious leaders mixed magic with official beliefs, like in Renaissance Christian Kabbalah, which combined Jewish mysticism and Catholic symbols. Similar blends happened elsewhere: Yoruba deities became Catholic saints in Cuban Santería, and Appalachian magic mixed Bible verses with old European charms.

"High" ceremonial and "folk" magics differed but also mingled:

Aspect	Folk Magic	High/Ceremonial Magic
Ritual Complexity	Simple, adaptable	Complex, formalized
Transmission	Oral, practical	Written, initiatory
Social Class	Everyday people	Elites and clergy
Example Practitioners	Cunning folk	Rosicrucian magicians

This table highlights the main differences between the two. Folk magic is accessible and flexible, while ceremonial magic is formal and exclusive.

Take John Dee as an example. He was a 16th-century scholar who advised Queen Elizabeth I by day and performed complex, ceremonial rituals by night to summon angels. In contrast, a 19th-century English wise woman might cure warts or nightmares with apples or Bible verses, using a simple, practical approach based on local needs. Marie Laveau of New Orleans, a free Black woman, blended Catholic and African practices and served her community as a healer and priestess, demonstrating adaptability and wisdom.

Marie Laveau's Everyday Mysticism

Marie Laveau's Voodoo brought together African, French, Spanish, and Indigenous traditions in Creole New Orleans. She went to Catholic Mass but also led rituals in Congo Square. Her influence came from linking community needs with old wisdom, healing with herbs, blessing amulets, and offering advice. Laveau adjusted traditions to fit her time, making magic a natural part of daily life in her community.

Political and religious oppression often forced magical practices into hiding or disguised them as customs. Practitioners used images from dominant religions, creating blended traditions such as African American "rootwork," and Appalachian "powwow," each composed of many influences.

Whether you recall lighting candles in church, hearing stories about saints, or seeing neighbors whisper protective words, you are part of these traditions. The urge to find meaning in ritual and to blend old practices with today's needs remains strong. It lives in anyone who shapes their world with intention or finds comfort in tradition during uncertain times.

Seasonal Rituals Across Traditions.

When you notice winter turning into spring or feel restless as summer ends, you are in tune with the rhythms that shape rituals around the world. The "Wheel of the Year" is a well-known model for seasonal spirituality, especially among modern Pagans and witches. Imagine the year as a circle with eight main festivals: Samhain, Yule, Imbolc, Ostara, Beltane, Litha, Lammas (Lughnasadh), and Mabon. Each one connects to nature's cycles and to questions like: How do we get through winter? When do we plant, harvest, rest, or celebrate? These festivals mark changes in the earth, help us keep track of time, build community, and encourage personal reflection.

Samhain's bonfires and honoring of ancestors mark both endings and new beginnings. Yule brings light to the longest nights, and Imbolc celebrates early signs of renewal, like snowdrops breaking through the frost or hope slowly returning. Ostara is about balance, with equal day and night, reflecting your own times of uncertainty or hope. Beltane is full of fire and fertility, encouraging celebration and planting seeds for the future. Litha, the height of the sun, is a time to celebrate and pause to notice achievements. Lammas, or Lughnasadh, is about gratitude for blessings and letting go of what you no longer need. Mabon, the autumn equinox, marks the end of the cycle with reflection and preparation for rest. Each festival is a marker, and its meaning can change and grow with you.

These cycles are not exclusive to Paganism. People in many cultures honor the changing seasons. In Jewish tradition, the calendar is used for more than just marking time. Passover in spring reflects nature's awakening, and Sukkot in autumn celebrates harvest and shelter. East Asian cultures have lunar festivals, such as the Mid-Autumn Festival, when families share mooncakes under the full moon. In Yoruba tradition, Egungun masquerades during the dry season invite ancestral spirits to bless the living. Customs may differ, but the main themes, renewal, gratitude, and remembrance, are shared by all.

Nature's calendar feels natural to us. Imbolc comes when winter is still present, but hope is growing; people might light candles or clean their homes to symbolize purification. In a city, this could mean clearing out clutter or opening windows on a cold morning to freshen your space. Lammas, when fields are complete, is a time to bake bread or share a meal in thanks. You do not need to live in the country; showing gratitude for your "harvest" can be cooking with local foods, writing thank-you notes, or noticing your achievements.

Spring rituals like Beltane often include outdoor fires and dancing, but you can adapt them even in small city spaces. Plant seeds or herbs on a balcony, and let each new sprout show your intentions. If you do not have outdoor space, you can create digital gardens and track your goals or creative projects in an app or journal as a modern way to plant. For solstices and equinoxes, make a digital altar by collecting seasonal images on your device, listening to music that matches the season, and setting reminders to notice the changing daylight. en spaces, you can tune into the season by walking through parks or neighborhoods, noting which trees bloom first, observing the shift of colors in street gardens, or simply pausing to feel the weather change as you go about your day. These small acts foster awareness and connect you quietly with nature's cycles amid urban life.

If you are secular or unsure about spiritual beliefs but still want ritual, focus on symbols. Light a candle for hope at Imbolc, let go of regrets at Samhain by burning or shredding notes, or invite friends to share a meal for Lammas. Ritual does not require belief; it helps mark time, change, and your story. The Wheel of the Year can always be adapted. No matter what you believe, the changing seasons invite you to join in this cycle of light, rest, and renewal.

Crossroads and Cross-Pollination Reveal How Traditions Intertwine

History is full of crossroads. When people, ideas, or beliefs meet, something new often appears, sometimes wild, sometimes beautiful, sometimes unusual. This happened during the Renaissance, when European scholars discovered ancient Hermetic texts from Egypt and Greece and combined them with Christian, Jewish, and Arabic wisdom. Artists began painting angels with alchemical symbols, and philosophers wrote about the unity of all things. The Hermetic revival was not just about copying old texts; it was about mixing magic, faith, and science into something new. This led to new rituals, new symbols, and a rise in magical thinking that influenced everything from poetry to architecture. This blending of traditions is even clearer in places like the Caribbean. In Cuba, Santería combines Yoruba deities from West Africa with Catholic saints, as enslaved Africans had to hide their faith within church rituals. Vodou in Haiti is similar: old gods are honored through the faces of saints, prayers mix French and African languages, and ceremonies use both drums and rosaries. These traditions are not fixed; they change, borrow, and survive by becoming something new. If you have ever wondered why a ritual feels layered, or why a Catholic candle is placed next to African cowrie shells, it is because people have always found ways to keep their traditions alive, even under pressure.

Theosophy in the 19th century brought a new kind of blending. Western seekers like Helena Blavatsky looked to the East for inspiration, drawing on Hindu and Buddhist ideas and blending them with Western occultism. Soon, Sanskrit words and chakras appeared in London parlors. This mix sparked interest in meditation, reincarnation, and astral travel among people who had never met a monk or a guru. Sometimes this was done with care, but other times it reduced deep traditions to a vague idea of "Eastern wisdom."

Blending traditions has created new religions, art movements, and even pop culture icons. Tarot, for example, began as a simple Italian card game. Over time, occultists assigned meanings to the cards, drawing on Egyptian gods and Kabbalistic paths, so that many now see Tarot as a miniature version of the universe. The pentagram is another example: it was a protective symbol in ancient Greece, later linked to Christian ideas about the five wounds of Christ, and is now a popular symbol for modern witches. The goddess Isis was once an Egyptian deity, but the Romans combined her with Greek goddesses and spread her worship. Symbols travel and gain new meanings wherever they go.

However, there is a downside to this creative borrowing. Sometimes magic becomes deeper and more interesting, but at other times it loses important elements like context, nuance, and respect for its origins. When powerful cultures take freely from others, especially those who have faced oppression, it can lead to distortion or erasure. For example, a Yoruba drum rhythm might become just background music in a yoga class, or an Indigenous smudge ritual might turn into a "wellness trend" with no real meaning. It is easy to oversimplify what is complex or forget the people behind these traditions.

This does not mean you should never explore traditions outside your own. Being curious about other cultures is natural and can be rewarding, but it takes mindfulness and honest effort. If you are interested in practices from another tradition, pause and ask yourself: Is it the symbolism, the ritual, or the sense of community or beauty that attracts you? Before you try something new, take time to learn its history. Who created it? What does it mean to the people who practice it? Is it open to outsiders, or is it private and sacred? Go beyond a quick online search, read books, listen to practitioners, and learn what is important about it.

What draws you to a practice outside your heritage?

Write about one practice or symbol from another culture that fascinates you. What feelings or questions does it stir up? What do you know about its source? How might you learn more, without just taking what appeals on the surface?

When blending traditions, respect their complexity. Borrow carefully, and appreciate differences as much as similarities. Magic grows at crossroads, but it is strongest when grounded in respect and genuine curiosity.

A Practical Toolkit for Cultural Appropriation vs. Respectful Engagement

When you explore magic or mysticism, you may find practices, symbols, or rituals that seem powerful and tempting, especially if they look beautiful, mysterious, or promise results. But not everything you see in a book or online is yours to use. Cultural appropriation happens when someone takes parts of another culture's spirituality, rituals, objects, or words without understanding their depth, context, or meaning for the people who practice them. This often involves a power imbalance. If you have not faced oppression for your beliefs and you take sacred elements from a group that has, you risk taking without consent or respect. This can turn something meaningful into just a trend, making it empty.

Power dynamics are important. Imagine seeing a ritual online, like a smudging ceremony or a dance, and thinking it looks fascinating or magical. If you copy it without knowing its background or who has the right to use it, you might be taking rather than honoring. Appropriation is not just using someone else's culture; it is taking parts out of context, often for personal gain or style, and ignoring who created it, who suffered for it, and what it means to them. Sometimes this happens out of excitement or curiosity, but good intentions do not prevent real harm. The difference between honoring and taking is about listening, learning, and asking fundamental questions before you start.

It is helpful to pause and think about your reasons. Here are some honest questions to guide you:

Am I honoring, or am I just taking?

Do I know the cultural or spiritual source of this practice?

Have I learned from people in the tradition, or only from secondhand sources?

Can I name who created this ritual, symbol, or tool, and do I know what it means to them?

Have I asked for permission or received advice from someone in the tradition?

Can I support living communities by buying from Indigenous authors, artists, or teachers rather than from big companies?

What would I do if someone from this culture asked me to stop? Would I listen?

These questions are not meant to shame you; they are to help you act with care and curiosity. If you feel defensive or unsure, take it as a sign to pause and learn more.

Respectful engagement is not about closing yourself off from learning; it is about building relationships and showing humility. There are many ways to do this well. Look for teachers and elders who welcome you. Go to open, public rituals where you are invited as a guest, listen more than you speak, and follow the community's rules. When buying spiritual tools or art, choose creators from that tradition. Read books by Indigenous authors, not just outsiders. If you are invited into a practice, ask what is open to outsiders and what is private. Show gratitude and give back when you can; do not just take what you like and leave. Being an ally means supporting living traditions with your money, your voice, and your time. Everyone makes mistakes, especially when starting. Maybe you bought a sacred item online and used it disrespectfully, like burning white sage without understanding its meaning or history. Perhaps you led a ritual at a friend's house and later learned the chants were only for initiated members of a closed community. If this happens, take responsibility. Apologize sincerely to those affected if you can, and stop using the practice until you learn more. Use the experience to educate yourself and others. Humility is essential; no one knows everything, and most tradition-keepers value honest effort more than perfection.

Checklist for Ethical Engagement

- Do I know the history and meaning of this practice?

- Am I using this with permission or guidance?

- Am I supporting living communities (financially or otherwise)?

- Have I sought out voices from within the tradition?

- Would I be comfortable explaining my use to someone from that culture?

- Am I willing to course-correct if I learn something new?

If in doubt, pause and research more.

For more education and support, look for organizations that focus on cultural preservation and stopping appropriation. Find books by Indigenous writers about spirituality; many offer online lectures or courses for respectful learners. Honest mistakes are part of learning; what matters is how you respond. This process builds trust with other cultures and with yourself as someone who wants to practice with respect and integrity.

Living Lineages for Connecting with Contemporary Communities

Magic and mysticism aren't museum pieces; they are alive and constantly changing in today's world. If you wonder whether these traditions are still active, look around. I once spoke with a member of the Hermetic Order who said their weekly study group was "half philosophy club, half experiment lab." The group focused on applying ancient teachings in real life, dealing with both doubts and breakthroughs. When I talked to a rootworker from the American South, what stood out was not the "spells" but how she described her practice as a mix of family recipes, ancestral stories, and neighborhood needs, a living tradition shaped by her own hands. A Zen teacher I met at a meditation center said that while his lineage goes back centuries, his teachings must connect with students who use smartphones and face modern stress. the sidelines, peering in from afar. If you want to experience these living lineages for yourself, there are more options than ever before. Local metaphysical shops often post flyers for public rituals or workshops. Hoodoo supply stores sometimes host classes or Q&A sessions open to anyone who wants to attend, ask questions, and see if it feels like a fit. Meditation sanghas, groups dedicated to mindfulness or Buddhist practice, welcome newcomers, often providing free or donation-based sessions. Online, the options are even broader: forums, Discord servers, private social media groups, and even Zoom classes with teachers from across the globe. Finding your people can be as simple as searching for local covens on Meetup or joining a virtual book club about mysticism.

When you reach out or join a group, good manners are important. Start by reading any posted guidelines or FAQs. Introduce yourself honestly and say if you are new to the tradition; most communities value humility over showing off. Listen before you speak, especially in groups with established customs. Do not rush to share your own experiences; watch how others interact first. Always ask before taking photos or recording events, and if you have questions, ask with genuine interest, not skepticism. Not every group will be right for you, and that is normal.

Discernment is essential; trust your instincts if something feels wrong. Healthy, magical, and mystical communities will welcome questions, personal choice, and boundaries. Watch out for warning signs like leaders who demand secrecy or unquestioning loyalty, groups that pressure you for money or personal information, or anyone who says their way is the only "true" path. Exploitation can appear as emotional manipulation or cult-like behavior. If you see cliques, gossip, or shaming of outsiders, consider leaving. Leaving a toxic group can feel awkward or scary, but your well-being comes first. Reach out to friends outside the group or online support if you need help leaving.

Being part of a living tradition is not just about receiving wisdom; it's about giving back and building something together. There are so many ways to contribute that don't require expertise or years of experience. Volunteering at public rituals, helping set up altars, clean up after ceremonies, or simply welcoming newcomers, strengthens community ties and gives you a deeper understanding of how traditions function in real life. Supporting tradition-aligned artists, herbalists, bookshops, and craftspeople keeps the culture vibrant and ensures money flows into the hands of those keeping these lineages alive. If you learn something meaningful from a teacher or elder, share it with proper attribution and gratitude, don't pass off others' insights as your own.

Knowledge grows when it is shared with care and purpose. You might organize a small reading group or host an online discussion about a favorite magical text. You could write thank-you notes to elders or creators who inspire you, or donate books to local libraries so others can learn too. Even recommending a good teacher or shop to someone interested helps keep valuable knowledge moving.

Living traditions thrive when people approach them with respect, curiosity, and generosity, not just as consumers, but as caretakers for the future. Magic is not only a private act; it lives in relationships and exchanges. When you show up honestly and take part in your community, in person or online, you help traditions grow and last for future generations.

This chapter has explored both the roots and branches of tradition, showing how it stays alive through real people, places, and conversations. As we move on to practical rituals and tools, remember that the wisdom you seek is both old and living, ready to meet you wherever you are.

Chapter Three

Rituals, Tools, and Sacred Space

A Step-by-Step Walkthrough to Craft Your First Ritual

Picture yourself in your kitchen at dusk, holding a mug and wanting a moment of clarity or a fresh start. That feeling is where ritual begins. You don't need special items or old-fashioned words, just a bit of structure and a willingness to be present. Ritual is for everyone, not just the mystical. It helps you mark a change, focus your mind, and bring meaning into your day.

Creating your first ritual is about making a process that fits you.

Step 1: Begin preparing by clearing your space and your mind. This signals that something important is about to happen. You might tidy up, light a candle, or take a few deep breaths. These simple actions help you become present. Preparation isn't about being formal; it's about being practical, removing distractions, and turning your focus inward.

Step 2: Set your intention. Think about what you want from this moment, like letting go of stress, welcoming new opportunities, or just taking time to appreciate life. Speak your intention out loud or write it down to make the moment clear and meaningful.

Step 3: Take action, which is the heart of the ritual. Pick a gesture that fits your goal. For new beginnings, you could light a candle or open a window for fresh air. Try a breathing exercise: breathe in new possibilities and breathe out what you want to let go. The action doesn't have to be big; it just needs to feel right for you.

Step 4: End the ritual with intention. Blow out the candle, close your journal, or say thank you. Finishing the ritual helps you feel grounded and makes it easier to return to your daily routine.

Here's a simple "New Beginnings" ritual you can do with everyday things. Start by cleaning your space, wiping a counter or shaking out a rug, and picture old energy leaving as you do. Stand with your feet flat on the floor to feel steady. Say your intention out loud: "I welcome new possibilities." Then, if it's safe, light a candle, or cup your hands and imagine a ball of light between them. Breathe in to invite something new, and breathe out to let go of worries. Repeat this a few times. When you're done, say "thank you" out loud or in your mind, or do what feels right. Put out the candle or slowly open your hands to let the energy go.

You can adjust every part of this ritual to fit your comfort and beliefs. Use words like "I'm open to new opportunities" if you prefer. Change the gestures if you want, or write your intention on a sticky note to carry with you.

Writing in a journal after your ritual can deepen the experience. It's not about whether something magical happened, but about noticing what you felt. What thoughts or feelings came up? Did you feel any resistance, surprise, or comfort? Let your thoughts flow without judging them; the most helpful insights come later.

Post-Ritual Checklist

- Was my focus steady or distracted?

- Did I feel at ease with each step?

- Did any part feel awkward or unnatural?

- What emotions or sensations arose?

- Do I feel lighter, more transparent, more inspired, or unchanged?

Don't stress about doing everything perfectly. Ritual isn't a performance or a test. Every time you try, you learn something new, and mistakes help you make the ritual your own. Even if nothing magical happens, feeling calmer or more present is valuable. Be kind and open with yourself as you try new things.

If you start to worry about whether you're doing it right, remember that everyone begins somewhere, and nobody is perfect every time. Even people with lots of experience forget words or laugh during rituals. These moments make your practice more personal and help you improve. Remind yourself: "I showed up for myself today." That's always a win.

Over time, you'll learn to trust your instincts when creating rituals. It's not about doing everything perfectly, but about honoring what feels right in each moment and letting yourself learn as you go.

Circle Casting in Small Spaces

Circle casting is often portrayed as grand and mysterious. Some say you need a vast room, a backyard, or a secret grove to do it right. In reality, you can create a powerful, protected ritual space even if you live in a tiny apartment or share a room. It's not about square footage or expensive tools. The core purpose is to focus your attention and set an energetic boundary, not to build a fortress. You're carving out a bubble of intention and presence, wherever you are. This helps you step outside the noise of daily life for a minute. You can do this without special incense or even candles.

You don't need to draw chalk lines on the floor or mark the cardinal directions with colored candles (though you absolutely can if you want and have the space). Visualization is just as valid. Close your eyes and picture a soft light forming a circle around you, like a gentle force field. If you're worried about neighbors or housemates peeking in, whisper your invocation or even say it silently in your mind. You can anchor your circle by placing an object at each corner, stones, buttons, or even folded socks if that's what you have on hand. A yoga mat or towel works as a symbolic boundary, helping your body feel contained. Roll it out and step onto it, knowing this is your spot for the next few minutes.

If you like techy solutions, use a meditation app to time your circle's "opening" and "closing." Set calming background noise to signal the start and end. Or pick a playlist that helps you focus. If you're practicing with friends remotely, agree on a time and cast your circles together via video call. Screens can serve as digital portals. Even a group chat can be a virtual sacred space. Everyone types out their intention, then hits send in unison.

Invisible circle casting is a clutch for privacy or when you need portability. Try tracing a small circle in the air with your finger. Nobody has to know what you're doing. Pocket stones make great boundary markers. Carry one in each pocket. As you settle in for your ritual, hold them and envision them "activating" a subtle circle around you. If words feel safer in your head than aloud, mentally repeat phrases like "This space is safe, and mine," or "Only what serves my highest good may enter." The real power comes from focused intent, not volume.

Privacy challenges pop up for almost everyone at some point. You might get interrupted by roommates, kids, or even the dog barking at the mail carrier. It helps to set expectations: hang a "do not disturb" sign or send a quick text to housemates saying, "Need ten minutes of quiet, please knock only for emergencies." If that's not possible, headphones are magic in themselves. Pop them on with white noise or soft music and let those sounds become your shield. Some people find that disruptions are less frustrating when they weave them into the ritual rather than fight them. If someone walks in mid-practice, pause and acknowledge it, maybe take a breath, then pick up where you left off or adapt on the fly.

Noise can be neutralized by background sounds such as rain, apps, wind chimes, or even a fan. These create coziness and blur out distractions. If you're interrupted and must stop, don't stress about breaking the "magic." Real life doesn't ruin ritual; sometimes it enhances it. You can adapt. Maybe you close your eyes for five seconds instead of five minutes. Perhaps you finish with a breath and a whispered thanks, then return to daily tasks.

Circle casting is for everyone, not only those with big houses or private gardens. You define your sacred space by what helps you feel present, focused, and safe. Every tiny effort to make room for yourself is valid. Your finger tracing, your whispered words, your mental boundary, they all count. The best circle is the one that fits your life right now. Let go of rules about what ritual "should" look like and trust what works for you. Magic becomes something you can carry anywhere, even in cramped or chaotic places.

Designing Sacred Space with What You Have

An altar doesn't need to be elaborate, permanent, or expensive. Its true purpose is to help ground your focus and create a connection. It serves as your ritual "charging dock" and a gathering place for your intentions. Whether simple or ornate, permanent or temporary, your altar is about you, not about impressing others. It is a personal spot to pause, reflect, and connect with what matters to you.

If you lack space for a dedicated altar, that's perfectly fine. There are countless creative ways to carve out sacred space, even in small, shared, or busy homes. A windowsill becomes an altar when you place a stone, candle, or small plant on it with intent. Nightstands work well, too. Set out a few objects that matter to you before bed. On a bookshelf, mix cherished keepsakes among your books. When you don't have space for anything permanent, try a "pop-up" altar, a tray or small box you can set up and put away as needed. Even your desk can become sacred for a few moments with a cup of tea, a scarf, and a favorite pen.

Digital altars are as valid as physical ones for many practitioners. Your phone wallpaper might be an inspiring or protective image. A Pinterest board full of uplifting images, symbols, and colors can serve as a portable altar. You might also use a digital notes app to collect affirmations and intentions. Sometimes, having your sacred items close by, digitally or otherwise, is more potent than anything on display.

You don't need to purchase special ritual gear; meaningful objects are often already at hand. Everyday items can hold deep significance when chosen intentionally. A ring from a loved one becomes a talisman for strength or protection. A pebble from a walk can have calming, grounding energy. Ordinary household candles, white or scented, are perfectly suitable for rituals; their power comes from your intention, not their price. Potted plants bring life to your altar, symbolizing growth and renewal. Even keys, coins, or cups can symbolize opportunity, abundance, or comfort.

Personal tokens have a place on your altar as well. Keep concert tickets from a special night, photos of loved ones, or a charm from a friend. A letter to yourself or a work badge can become sacred by intention. The meaning you assign to these objects far outweighs any traditional rule or expectation.

Keep your altar physically and energetically clean as part of self-care. Dust can gather quickly, especially in active homes. Wipe surfaces with a soft cloth regularly to show your items respect. Rearranging your altar refreshes its energy; notice what feels right and move things as needed. If anything feels heavy or stale, remove it and see how the atmosphere shifts.

Energetic cleansing doesn't require sage or incense, especially if those feel inaccessible or inappropriate. Simple breathwork works wonders: exhale over your altar, envisioning any heaviness dissipating. Ringing a bell sends vibrations through your space, breaking up stagnant energy. If that's not possible, use intention alone: hover your hands and imagine light filling the objects. Some people whisper small words of gratitude or encouragement as they tidy up.

Treat sacred objects with gentle respect. Handle them mindfully, appreciating their texture and weight. When bringing something new into your space, pause to "introduce" it by stating its significance, reinforcing its place in your practice. If you store altar items between rituals, wrap them or store them in a special box to protect and honor them.

Your sacred space can be whatever and wherever you need it to be, a surface transformed into an altar through care and intention. Designing this space isn't about rules; it's about tuning in to what grounds and inspires you, whether that's sunlight on a ring, the quiet presence of an old photo, or a flickering candle.

A Minimalist's Guide to Magical Essentials

When thinking about ritual tools, it's easy to get distracted by endless "must-have" lists and images of shelves packed with special objects. But what matters most is the meaning you assign to each tool, not its cost or traditional appearance. Ritual tools serve to symbolize and anchor your intentions, helping you shift your mind into a focused state. The classic set includes: a wand, a chalice, an athame, a pentacle, incense, and candles. Each has a symbolic role, but none are required for meaningful practice.

The wand channels intention and willpower; the chalice symbolizes receptivity, holding dreams or desires. The athame, or ritual knife, signifies clarity and boundaries, "cutting away" what isn't needed. The pentacle (a disc with a star) grounds your ritual and connects to the earth. Incense transforms air, shifting energy and carrying wishes, while candles bring literal and symbolic light, offering warmth and representing new beginnings.

You don't need textbook versions of these tools. Most people don't have ornate chalices or silver knives lying around. Everyday items work perfectly: a spoon can be a wand, your favorite mug a chalice, and a kitchen knife (handled with care) an athame. For a pentacle, a flat stone, a large button, or a coin will do. Incense can be a drop of essential oil on a tissue, a sprig of rosemary, or just an open window. Any candle works, tea lights, birthday candles, or jars, pick what's safe and feels right.

Everyday items often make rituals more personal and meaningful. Using a mug or a found stone brings your story and energy into your practice; magic feels more alive when tools come from your own life, not just a store.

There are practical reasons too. Specialized tools can quickly get expensive. Thrifted or upcycled items save money and add character. Objects with history, like a grandmother's spoon or a beach shell, carry more personal energy than something new. Making your own tools, like carving a wand from a fallen branch or drawing a pentacle on cardboard, adds creative energy. Personalizing tools with paint, yarn, symbols, or beads makes them truly yours.

Sustainability also matters. Take only what you need from nature, with gratitude. Avoid harvesting endangered plants or harming habitats. Use reusable, biodegradable materials: store herbs in glass jars, repurpose old cloth for altar cloths, and use beeswax candles instead of paraffin, if possible. This eco-friendly approach deepens your connection to nature and grounds your magic.

Privacy may shape how you select or disguise your tools. If you need to stay discreet, choose items that blend into your daily life, wear jewelry as a talisman, and keep your "wand" with kitchen utensils. Tools don't need to look magical; their power comes from your intention and use.

Making tools that reflect your identity and values is a creative act. You might make a staff from driftwood and decorate it with charms, craft pocket charms from clay or wire, or paint your pentacle in colors that inspire you. Tuck handwritten intentions inside candle holders or add meaningful symbols to any tool to turn something ordinary into something magical.

"What objects already in your life hold power or meaning for you, and how might they be used as ritual tools or symbols?"

Spend five minutes listing things charged with memory or emotion, like a shell from last summer, a lucky coin, or a comforting mug. Next time you need focus or ritual, experiment with bringing one of these objects into your space and see how it changes the experience.

Building your toolkit this way is about self-trust and creativity, not perfection. Every tool is as powerful as the intention and care you give it.

What to Do When Things Don't Go as Planned

No matter how much you prepare, reality loves to toss a surprise into even the most thoughtfully arranged ritual. Maybe you trip over your words, the candle won't light, or your mind starts wandering right when you want to feel most present. Sometimes you forget a key step or lose focus. Maybe someone barges in, your phone rings, or you suddenly feel awkward. Other times, everything goes fine technically, but you're left wondering if anything "magical" happened at all. These moments are universal. If you find yourself thinking, "Did I mess this up?" you're actually doing something right. Ritual isn't about rigid perfection; it's a living process shaped by everything you bring to it.

Anticipating the unexpected makes rituals more honest and resilient. Interruptions, distractions, or even total blanks are part of the experience. So, if a ritual feels flat or takes a left turn, try not to panic or judge yourself harshly. These are not failures. They're invitations to get curious about what's really happening, and often, they teach you more than when everything runs smoothly.

When things don't go as planned, pause and check in with yourself using a quick diagnostic checklist:

- Was your intention clear to you, or did it feel fuzzy or forced?

- Did you feel physically comfortable and emotionally ready, or was there an underlying discomfort, tension, or anxiety?

- Were there distractions, either from your environment or from inside your own mind, that pulled you away from the moment?

- If something interrupted you, did you adapt naturally or freeze up?

These questions aren't about assigning blame; they're about understanding what actually shaped your experience.

Actionable solutions help you keep moving forward, even if your ritual temporarily falls apart. If you forget a step or get interrupted, pause and breathe. Sometimes restarting the ritual from wherever you left off works. Other times, you might choose to close the ritual early, thank yourself for showing up, and save the rest for another time. If your location suddenly feels wrong, maybe roommates come home or the vibe shifts, don't be afraid to pick up and move elsewhere, even mid-ritual. Use humor when things go sideways. Laughing at a toppled candle or a mispronounced word reminds you that magic is alive and human, not some uptight performance.

Adapting rituals "on the fly" is not cheating. It's an act of creativity and self-care. If you planned on using a particular object but can't find it, substitute another that feels right in the moment. When words don't come, sit quietly and let your intention be silent instead. If an interruption breaks your focus, acknowledge it, maybe even weave it into your ritual by writing down what happened or turning it into a symbol of adaptability.

Reflective learning turns every hiccup into an opportunity for growth and self-discovery. After each ritual, smooth or messy, take a few minutes to jot down what worked well and what you might change next time. Maybe rituals at night feel more focused than ones in the morning. Maybe interruptions always happen at certain hours. Can you shift your timing in the future? Patterns often reveal themselves over weeks or months rather than in single sessions.

Celebrate even the most minor victories: showing up despite chaos, returning to your intention after a distraction, or simply finishing what you started. Each time you adapt rather than give up, you build resilience and self-trust. Some of my most memorable rituals have been the messy ones, the ones that refused to match my plans and instead taught me how to let go of control.

Ritual Rescue Checklist

- Was I clear about my purpose?

- Did I feel comfortable and present?

- What distractions popped up (internal or external)?

- How did I respond to surprises?

- What part of this ritual still felt nourishing?

- What would I try differently next time?

Tracking these details over time helps refine not just your rituals but also your own self-awareness. You'll notice which environments support focus and which times of day work best for you. Over time, noticing these patterns lets you shape rituals that truly fit your life, rather than struggling against what's "supposed" to work.

In closing this chapter, remember that magic doesn't need perfection; it thrives on authenticity and adaptability. Every attempt adds value, even when things don't go as planned. Trust that these experiences are part of building something real and personal.

As we move forward, keep this attitude of flexibility close at hand. The next chapter will help you deepen your practice with grounding and protection techniques, as well as practical ways to keep your magical life steady, even when the outside world is anything but predictable.

Chapter Four

Practices for Grounding, Protection, and Safe Exploration

Grounding Techniques for Urban, Indoor, or Nature-Deprived Practitioners

You know that feeling, scattered thoughts, tense body, and a sense of floating through your day? It's the opposite of grounded. Grounding brings you back to your body and the present, creating stability and clarity. Energetically, it means releasing excess energy and reconnecting to a steady source, like plugging into a power source. Psychologically, it calms anxiety and slows racing thoughts. Physically, it's noticing your heartbeat, breath, and feet on the floor. It's not magic; it's self-regulation with a mystical touch. Contrary to popular belief, grounding doesn't require being barefoot outdoors. City dwellers, apartment folks, and indoor workers can ground deeply, no patch of earth needed.

Start by ditching any guilt over not having access to nature. You can ground powerfully in a high-rise building, on public transport, or even in a windowless office. The trick is to find ordinary objects and simple actions that anchor you in your body and environment.

One of my favorite indoor grounding methods is the "floor touch" meditation:

1. Kick off your shoes and plant your bare feet on whatever flooring you've got (hardwood, tile, linoleum, or even plain old carpet).

2. Notice the temperature and texture beneath your toes.

3. Spread your weight from heel to ball. Wiggle your toes if you want.

4. Inhale slowly and imagine any static tension draining downward into the floor.

5. You don't need grass or roots. Just focus on contact and let your awareness move from head to toe.

If you can't stand, try this:

1. Choose a heavy object, such as a mug, stone, or spoon.

2. Hold it in both hands.

3. Pay attention to its hard, cool, or heavy qualities.

4. Feel your muscles respond to its weight.

5. If your thoughts start to spiral, press a cold water bottle to your palm as an interruption.

To use a wall for grounding:

1. Locate a sturdy surface.

2. Stand or sit with your back or shoulders against it.

3. Notice the solid support; let it remind you that you are physically present and stable.

4. If sitting, press your spine to the wall or seat back.

5. Try pressing your hands to your thighs as an added anchor.

Public spaces make grounding tricky; nobody wants to do a ritual in front of coworkers or strangers. That's where stealth helps. On public transit or at your desk, try closing your eyes or lowering your gaze. Visualize roots growing from your feet through the floor. The roots can be light, smoke, or vines, whatever fits. Let them stretch downward to connect with an inner calm. With each exhale, send stress out through the roots. With each inhale, draw up steadiness and clarity.

Another quick fix is rhythmic tapping or squeezing. Use a stress ball, tap your fingertips together under the table, or press your thumb to each finger in sequence. If you lose focus during a meeting, ground yourself by noticing sensory details: five things you can see, four you can touch, three you hear, two you smell, and one you can taste. This brief inventory quietly brings you back to the present.

If anxiety rises at work or in public, focus on slow breathing. Inhale for four counts and pause. Exhale for six counts. Imagine each breath as a wave washing out tension. Repeat a silent mantra like "Here now" or "Steady" if words help anchor you.

Grounding Effectiveness Log

Try tracking which techniques work best for you over the next week. Each day, jot down:

- How grounded do I feel right now? (Rate 1-10)

- Which method did I try? (Floor touch, mug anchor, wall-leaning, visualization, sensory inventory)

- How long did I practice?

- What changed in my mood or body?

- What surprised me?

Sample prompt for your journal: "When did I last feel scattered or ungrounded? What helped me come back?" Over time, patterns will emerge. Maybe wall-leaning soothes work stress, but tactile anchors work better at home.

There's no gold medal for doing grounding "right." What matters is paying attention and being willing to experiment until something clicks for you. Indoors or outdoors, surrounded by chaos or alone in silence, you always have access to grounding practices that bring you back home to yourself.

Simple Methods for Home and Self to Cleanse and Purify

Energetic cleansing is more than tidying up or washing before a meal. It's about intentionally clearing the invisible "static," or unseen lingering energy, from our spaces, belongings, and bodies. This static refers to the subtle, often negative energy that accumulates after arguments, illness, tough weeks, or when you feel weighed down or unfocused. For example, it can manifest as tension in a room after a difficult conversation. It can also feel like an oppressive atmosphere in a bedroom after poor sleep. Encounters, rituals, and emotional moments can all leave behind this energetic residue. Cleansing is a method to reset yourself and your surroundings. It is much like opening windows after a long winter, but for your spirit.

Cleansing doesn't need to be dramatic. You don't need smoke or rare herbs. Many effective tools are at hand. Sound is powerful; ring a bell in a heavy-feeling room, or, if you don't have one, clap in corners, behind doors, or under beds. Even upbeat music, singing bowls, or white noise can help shake things loose; the key is letting sound move through the space.

Water is another versatile ally. Washing your hands with full attention, focusing on the coolness and sensation, can become a cleansing ritual. Imagine the water carrying away emotional residue. To clear a room, fill a spray bottle with water, optionally adding a pinch of salt or a drop of safe essential oil, and lightly mist the air while visualizing negativity dissolving. A hint of lemon also refreshes the space. Out-breathing toward the floor or an open window gives unwanted energy a clear exit.

If you can't take physical action, use visualization. Imagine standing under a waterfall or a rain of light washing away residue from head to toe. Picture heaviness draining away and leaving you lighter. Cleanse objects by picturing them in sunlight or a gentle current.

Personalize rituals with what you have to boost confidence. Make a saltwater spray by dissolving a little salt in water, then mist doorways, windows, or your hands after meeting someone. For cleansing on the go, carry a small stone, tissue, or a cotton ball with essential oil. When weighed down, rub the stone, wipe hands thoughtfully, and inhale the scent for a quick refresh.

You don't need elaborate purchases or fixed recipes. Start with what feels right. Revise your approach as you discover what helps you most. Pay attention to what makes a space feel clear. Is it fresh air, a particular scent, shifting the furniture, or opening a window? Sometimes a simple change in airflow is all it takes.

Traditional methods like burning sage or palo santo have spiritual and environmental concerns. Both are overharvested and sacred in Indigenous cultures. If they're not part of your heritage, consider skipping them out of respect and care for the earth. There are alternatives: burn kitchen rosemary, crumble bay leaves at doorways, or place cinnamon sticks on windowsills for cleansing and protection without the concerns.

Source herbs locally when possible for ethical reasons. Rosemary from the grocery store, dried orange peels, or mint leaves from your garden work well. If fire or smoke isn't allowed, use herbs in sachets. Simmer them for steam or wave them while stating your intention. The effect is still powerful.

Fire-free methods are often safest and least noticeable. Sound and water don't trigger smoke alarms. Breathwork and visualizations don't draw unwanted attention. Saltwater sprays are gentle on sensitivities and beliefs. What matters is intention, not performance.

Let practicality guide your rituals; don't fret about perfection. If you want to mark the end of illness or conflict, wash all bedding and towels. Mentally bid goodbye to lingering energy as you load the washer. After arguments, clap in each corner and picture peace returning with each sound. Before meditation or reading tarot cards, wipe your table with lemon water or use your pocket kit.

Energetic cleansing is both magical and straightforward. It is woven into daily life by water, sound, scent, and intention. With each breath, each sweep of air or sound, you become lighter. Resetting, rather than letting heaviness linger, turns ordinary routines into anchors for well-being and self-trust.

Setting Boundaries for Energetic and Emotional Protection

"Setting boundaries" often comes up in self-help. In everyday life and magic, boundaries go deeper than social rules. They're about proactive self-care, similar to putting on sunscreen before heading outside. Boundaries keep your energy, emotions, and focus from getting tangled up in others' drama, moods, or expectations. Though invisible, they powerfully shape how you move through your day. You'll notice the need for boundaries if you leave a conversation feeling drained, scroll social media and suddenly grow irritable or anxious, or snap at minor annoyances for no reason. Other signs include sudden exhaustion or replaying someone else's bad mood long after you part. Sometimes called "sponging," this means absorbing emotions not your own. Nothing is wrong with you; it just means your energy filter needs reinforcement.

Setting boundaries doesn't have to be complicated or dramatic. Simple practices like visualization and intention can help. For example, try the "bubble of light." Imagine yourself enveloped in a soft, protective sphere of light. Choose any color that feels safe. See this bubble as permeable, welcoming in what nourishes you (like warmth and laughter) but turning away what drains or harms. Vivid imagery makes this exercise more effective, but even a basic sense or intention is helpful. Similarly, try the mirror shield: envision a reflective surface facing outward from your body, reflecting negativity rather than absorbing it. Practice this before entering crowds or challenging meetings. Even repeating a quick phrase, like "What is mine stays with me, what is not passes through," can clarify boundaries.

Boundaries aren't just about energy work; they're reflected in your daily habits and choices, too. When facing draining environments, like family gatherings or workplace drama, get practical. Set limits for conversations you know sap your energy; decide how long you'll attend an event or how promptly you'll respond to texts. Small physical cues can reinforce your intentions: crossing your arms, stepping back during tense moments, or wearing a favorite piece of jewelry as a "shield." Clothing and jewelry can serve as subtle signals to yourself that you're protected and in charge. Sometimes a simple "no" or "I need a breather" is the most effective boundary. This might feel uncomfortable, especially if you're used to being a people-pleaser, but it's an act of self-respect. Remember, you don't owe anyone unlimited access to your energy.

When your boundaries are challenged, and they will be, it's important to know how to repair and reinforce them. After a draining day or tough interaction, check in with yourself. Journaling can help clarify where your energy has been depleted. Try asking, "Where did I give away my energy today?" Write freely; maybe it was during a tense meeting or by listening to a friend vent for too long. Identifying these moments gives you insight for next time. If writing isn't your thing, do a "closing the gate" ritual: sit or stand quietly, imagine any open doors in your energy field gently swinging shut, and tell yourself, "I call my energy back." You can also mimic locking a door or drawing curtains, any small, physical act that helps you feel settled.

Physical resets are undervalued but effective for boundary repair. After social events or stressful days, washing your hands intentionally, feeling the water rinse away what isn't yours, can help. Changing clothes when you get home signals to your body that the outside world is now at a distance. Many people find it helpful to brush themselves off from head to toe, like dusting off invisible residue. A quick shake of your limbs or light stretching also helps clear stuck energy and emotions.

Over time, you'll spot patterns: certain people or situations reliably poke holes in your boundaries, while others leave you feeling upbeat and safe. Awareness is key; it helps you adjust without guilt or the need to explain yourself to those who don't understand. There's no place for fear-based thinking; boundaries aren't rigid walls but flexible frameworks that let you stay open to what matters while keeping out what doesn't serve you. If your boundaries get breached, it doesn't mean you're "bad" at setting them; it simply means you're human and learning what works for you.

You might fear seeming cold or unfriendly by enforcing boundaries, but in fact, healthy boundaries make a genuine connection possible. They let you show up as your true self, instead of acting as an emotional sponge or chameleon. People who respect your boundaries will also respect you more, and if someone doesn't, that's a valuable signal about the supportiveness of that relationship. If boundaries are new or intimidating for you, start small: say one clear "no," intentionally exit one uncomfortable situation, or take a day to check in with yourself before saying yes to extra commitments.

Boundaries are dynamic; they grow, stretch, and sometimes need repair as life knocks into them. Practicing boundary-setting and repair helps you more easily notice what feels right and what doesn't. Self-awareness is your best ally: if something feels off, pause and ask yourself what you need right now to feel safe and whole again.

Self-Assessment Checkpoints with Journaling and Reflective Safety Tools

When you're mixing magic or mystical practice into daily life, stopping to check in with yourself is like putting on a seatbelt before driving. Self-assessment isn't flashy, but it's the safety net that keeps your feet on the ground and your head clear. This isn't just about avoiding drama or mishaps; it's about staying honest with what you need and where you are, physically, emotionally, mentally, and energetically. I find that when I pause to notice what's happening inside me before any ritual or meditation, I learn more about what's actually going on. That can mean the difference between a practice that feels nourishing and one that leaves you feeling off-balance or disappointed. Creating a personal check-in routine helps you tune into yourself, spot red flags early, and build real confidence, not just wishful thinking.

A simple template helps organize the chaos.

Before you start any ritual or even a moment of quiet intention, try asking yourself: How does my body feel right now? Are you tense, tired, jittery, hungry?

Next, get honest about your emotional state. Are you angry, sad, content, numb, or something else? Energetically, do you feel charged up, flat, scattered, or heavy?

Finally, scan your mind: Are your thoughts racing, focused, or foggy? This isn't about judgment; it's just information, like checking the weather before heading outside.

If you want to keep it all in one place, jot the answers into a journal or a notes app. Over time, these logs become a map of your magical rhythm.

Readiness for practice is not always apparent. Sometimes we push ourselves to meditate, cast a spell, or journal through a rough patch because we think we "should," even if we're wiped out or emotionally raw. Before starting anything, ask: Am I rested? Have I eaten or had enough water? Is my mind in a place where I can focus? Am I feeling pressured to perform or genuinely curious about exploring today? If you catch yourself going through the motions out of obligation or FOMO (fear of missing out), that's a signal to pause. Maybe a walk, a snack, or just a nap will serve you better than any ritual right now. The magic is in listening.

Afterward, don't skip the reflection. Spend a few minutes noting what happened, what felt good, what felt weird or awkward. Did your energy shift in any way? Did you get distracted or zone out? Maybe you felt lighter after, a small win worth celebrating. Or maybe nothing happened at all, and you're left with more questions than answers. That's valuable too; sometimes what doesn't work is as revealing as what does. Tracking these patterns over time, like how certain practices affect your mood, energy level, sleep, or focus, shows you where your strengths are and where something needs tweaking. It also guards against getting stuck in routines that no longer serve you.

It's easy to miss subtle warning signs when you're excited to try something new. Pay attention when certain practices consistently leave you feeling depleted rather than restored. Persistent fatigue, headaches that don't budge, intrusive thoughts that get louder after ritual work, these are not badges of honor but signals to slow down. Anxiety that lingers or deepens isn't something to "power through." Instead of blaming yourself for being "not spiritual enough," these are moments to ask: What boundaries do I need before next time? Do I need more rest, better nutrition, or just time away from certain practices? Sometimes the best move is to step back and reevaluate rather than push forward.

If you hit a wall, feelings of dread before practice, recurring nightmares after certain meditations, or emotional intensity that feels unmanageable, it's time to ask for help outside your own toolbox. Consider reaching out to a therapist experienced with spiritual issues (many are open to this conversation), an experienced mentor in your tradition who won't guilt-trip you for needing space, or even supportive friends who understand your path. There's no shame in pausing your practice when things get rough; real growth comes from knowing when to rest and when to seek more support.

Safety Net Journal Prompts

Try these questions before and after practice:

- What is my body telling me right now?

- What emotion is most present?

- Where is my energy level (high/low/neutral)?

- Do I genuinely want this, or am I forcing it?

- What shifted for me during/after this practice?

- Did anything feel off or uncomfortable?

- What do I need before next time (rest, food, boundaries)?

- Who could I reach out to if I needed help processing?

If any answer raises concern, especially persistent fatigue or anxiety, consider contacting local therapists who understand spiritual matters (many list this as an area of focus), reaching out to crisis support lines if needed, or seeking mentors through reputable community networks.

Self-assessment is an ongoing practice; the more you do it, the more intuitive it becomes. You start noticing patterns. Maybe full moon rituals leave you energized, but group meditations drain you; maybe winter makes introspection harder, but easier to ground physically. Each log entry builds self-trust. You don't need to be perfect or have all the answers. You need to be honest about where you are and be willing to adjust as needed.

This chapter has covered how grounding, cleansing, boundaries, and self-reflection keep your magical life safe and sustainable. These aren't restrictions; they're ways to make sure what works for others actually works for you. As we move forward, keep this sense of curiosity and care close by. Up next: we'll explore how to shape rituals and practices that grow with you, adapting as your needs and interests change over time.

Chapter Five

Modular, Adaptable, and Beginner-Safe Rituals for Daily Life

The Five-Minute Ritual for Magic and Busy Schedules

Have you ever had just five minutes before your next task, like a Zoom call, picking up the kids, or when your alarm rings? We all want more time, but life doesn't always give it to us. That's why I want to show you how a little magic can fit into five minutes or less. It's not about rushing, but about taking a focused pause that works with your busy day. Ritual isn't about how many candles you light or how long you meditate. What matters most is intention: choosing to be present for yourself and shift your mindset, even if it's just for a breath or a song.

A ritual consists of a few key parts: intention, action, a symbolic gesture, and closure. It doesn't have to be complicated. A five-minute practice takes these elements and makes them fit your schedule. Intention is the most important part; with it, even a single breath can make a difference. These short practices are like quick boosts for your spirit, brief but effective.

Let's get practical with three quick ritual templates for different needs. You can change them, swap steps, or add your own ideas. For "Morning Alignment," start with a deep breath and set an intention for your day, like "I greet challenges with curiosity." Add a gesture, such as stretching your arms overhead or touching your heart. For a "Desk Reset," close your eyes, let go of tension, and place your hands on your desk or lap. Say a grounding word like "focus" or "steady," then tap your fingers three times to lock in that feeling before you get back to work. "Evening Release" is helpful when you're stressed at night: sit comfortably, breathe out slowly, and picture your worries melting away. Make a simple movement to let go, like shaking out your hands or wiping them on your jeans. Finish by feeling grateful for anything that went well today, even if it's something small.

These rituals work best when you connect them to daily transition points, the moments when one part of life shifts into another. Waking up, before a big meeting, after dinner, or right before sleep are all natural thresholds where your energy resets. Every time you move from one "mode" to another, you have an opening to pause and claim a moment for yourself. Even if all you do is take two mindful breaths with intention at those points, you're building a magical practice that adapts to real life.

The great thing about five-minute rituals is their flexibility. You don't need any special items; anything meaningful to you can be a tool. If you want more energy, pick a bold color, like wearing red socks or holding a bright mug. If you need confidence before a tough call, stand in a strong pose with your feet planted, chest open, and hands on your hips. You can also create your own hand motion for your goal, like pressing your palms together for unity or drawing an infinity sign in the air for creativity. Add affirmations like "I am resilient" or "I welcome insight," or use objects that matter to you, such as a lucky coin, a scarf from someone you care about, or your favorite pen.

Create Your Personal Five-Minute Ritual Menu

Spend a few minutes thinking about times in your day when a little magic would help, like a hard morning, feeling tired in the afternoon, or getting ready for bed. For each of these times, try this simple process:

- An intention (what do you want to feel or invite?),

- A gesture or action (stretching, tapping, holding an object),

- End with a word or affirmation, such as "done," "thank you," or "release."

- Try using colors or objects that help your mood.

Create at least two rituals: one to help you feel grounded and one to boost your energy. Write them down somewhere you'll notice them.

Rituals don't have to be complicated. The most powerful moments are usually personal   and straightforward. As you use these rituals in your daily life, before sleep, between emails, or after hearing tough news, you'll notice how much intention matters. With time, you'll create your own toolkit for handling busy or uncertain times.

Invisible Spells for Subtle Practice in Work and Public Spaces

Something is exciting about practicing magic when no one around you notices. Invisible spells are great for keeping your practice private, whether you're at work, on the subway, in a coffee shop, or around people who might not understand. You don't need props, fancy words, or even any visible movement. The real magic is in your focus and how you quietly direct your energy. Visualization, silent intention, and small gestures all work. These private techniques can feel even more powerful because they're just for you. You might create a sense of calm in a stressful meeting or send warmth to a friend just by thinking of them. You don't need to be loud or obvious, just present and intentional.

Let's get practical with examples. Picture yourself on crowded public transit: headphones in, eyes on your phone, but inside, you're building an "energy shield." Visualize a sphere of light around your body, maybe it glows blue or gold, or it feels cool and steady, deflecting tension and negativity from the packed car. Nobody sees a thing, but you're holding boundaries that keep you grounded. If a coworker is driving you up the wall, try a silent blessing instead of gritting your teeth. As you listen to them talk, imagine sending a gentle wave of patience or kindness their way; you might picture a soft light connecting you both, or repeat a phrase in your head like, "May you find ease." It sounds simple, but these small acts can shift your whole day.

Sigils are another way to practice invisible magic. These are symbols filled with your intention, drawn where only you know. You can trace one on your palm with your finger while waiting for a meeting, or draw it in the air above your notebook before writing. You don't need ink or paper; just the movement and your intention are enough. Even playing with a pen can be spellwork: before a big presentation, hold your pen and imagine it filling with confidence or clarity, then use it as your "magic wand" as you write or gesture. This act is private, but it can make you feel more empowered.

It's important to feel safe and comfortable when practicing subtle magic, especially when others might judge or misunderstand. The key is to blend your ritual into everyday actions so it doesn't stand out. For example, when stirring your coffee, turn the spoon clockwise to invite good energy or counterclockwise to let go of stress; no one will notice. Tying your shoes can be a chance to add protection: as you tie the laces, imagine securing your day with steadiness and focus. Even small actions like adjusting your jewelry, brushing your hair aside, or tapping your foot can hold intention if you want them to.

Sometimes blending invisible magic into daily life means letting go of traditional forms and trusting your own instincts. If you're worried someone will catch on, keep things even subtler: run through a visualization while looking out the window or set intentions during a restroom break. Your privacy is important; nobody needs to know that tying your scarf is actually a mini-spell for comfort, or that the way you stack your papers is laced with wishes for clarity.

Your Invisible Spell Log

Use a notebook or notes app to track each time you practice invisible magic this week. Write down what you did, how you felt before and after, and if anyone noticed (they probably didn't). At the end of the week, look back:

- Which invisible spells felt good, became easy, or felt awkward?

- Did your mood, confidence, or interactions change?

Use your notes to keep what works, adjust what doesn't, and remember that even small acts matter.

Invisible magic works best when you experiment and have fun with it. You'll find that some actions make you feel strong and calm, while others might not feel right, and that's okay. Over time, these minor spells will become part of your daily routine, giving you a private sense of confidence and calm wherever you go.

Coffee Consecrations and Commuter Meditations to Bring Magic into the Mundane

Think about your first cup of coffee or tea in the morning, the steam rising, the warmth in your hands, the smell that tells you it's time to start the day. Most people rush through this without noticing. But what if you paused and made it a special moment? Everyday routines you barely notice can become powerful rituals if you bring new intention to them. You don't need a special day or a fancy altar; your kitchen counter or car seat is enough. The magic begins when you treat the ordinary as a chance for something meaningful.

Making your morning drink special is simple and can really change how you feel. Before you take your first sip, hold your mug with both hands and close your eyes for a moment. Imagine golden light swirling into your drink, or see the surface shine as you inhale its scent. Say or think a phrase like, "Let this coffee bring me focus," or "May this tea calm me." If you want, make up your own words: "May this cup give me courage and patience for the day." You can also draw a symbol on your mug with your finger, or stir it clockwise for energy and counterclockwise for calm. It's not about saying the perfect thing; it's about connecting with what you need right then.

You can use food rituals too. Before eating breakfast or lunch, pause and look at your plate. Silently thank everyone who helped bring you this food, even if it's just you heating leftovers. Set an intention for nourishment, like "Let this meal give me energy" or "May I feel supported by this food." For snacks, touch the wrapper or container and take a breath before opening it, focusing on gratitude or a wish. These small acts aren't about guilt; they're simple ways to ground yourself, be present, and listen to what your body and spirit need.

Commuting often feels like the least magical part of the day. Whether you're stuck in traffic, crowded on a bus, or walking in the rain, it's easy to zone out. But you can turn this time into a ritual with a simple mindset shift. Your commute isn't wasted, it's a chance for ritual. Before you leave home, imagine a gentle bubble of protection around you, a shield that moves with you. If you're walking, match your breath to your steps: inhale for four steps, exhale for four. With each inhale, imagine bringing in calm; with each exhale, let go of tension. If you're driving or on transit, use stops or red lights as reminders for short mantras like "Safe and steady," "Clear path ahead," or "I move through obstacles with ease." You can tap your fingers on the steering wheel or seat in time with these words.

You can go beyond breathwork and visualizing bubbles. Pick a "magic object" before you leave home, like a lucky coin, a ring from someone important, or even a pen you love to use. Keep it in your pocket or bag and squeeze it whenever you need a boost of confidence or protection. This object becomes a reminder that you carry intention and control with you all day.

Turning routines into rituals can change your mood faster than any self-help tip I've tried. When I started blessing my coffee in the morning, I felt less rushed, even on days I left the house in a hurry. My commute became less stressful and more about checking in with myself. The change isn't always huge; sometimes it's just a steady or clear feeling that lasts all day.

Mundane-to-Magical Ritual

Try this tonight: use a notebook or notes app to write down which everyday routines you added a little magic to today, like coffee, meals, or commuting. How did it feel to bring magic into these moments? Did your mood, focus, or patience change? Did any object become a secret good luck charm? Try new words or gestures tomorrow. Over time, you'll find which rituals work best for you and see how much magic is hidden in your daily routine.

The more you add intention and presence to your daily habits, the more empowered and connected you'll feel, even when life doesn't seem special or magical. Making the ordinary magical isn't about avoiding reality; it's about being there for yourself, just as you are, and finding real strength in the middle of everyday life.

Adapt Lunar Rituals to Your Life with Moon Cycles in a Modern World

You don't need dramatic settings or rituals to feel the moon's influence. For centuries, moon phases have shaped people's routines, and you can still connect with them, even if you look out your window. Each phase, new, waxing, full, and waning, reflects different moods and intentions. The new moon is a time to start fresh and set new goals. As the moon grows, build momentum and confidence. The full moon is for celebrating, showing gratitude, or finishing things. When the moon wanes, let go of what you don't need, tidy up, or slow down. These are gentle reminders for self-reflection, not strict rules.

Modern lunar rituals can be practical and straightforward. You don't need anything fancy; minimalist rituals work just as well as big ceremonies. At the new moon, set an intention and write down a habit, mindset, or goal on your phone or a sticky note. Or light a candle and think about your intention for a few moments; you don't need circles or chants unless you want them. For the full moon, focus on letting go: write down what you want to release and then destroy or delete it, or clean out old photos or emails. Even small actions can lift your mood.

You don't have to match your schedule perfectly to the lunar calendar. Life gets busy, and sometimes you'll miss a phase because of work or other things. That's okay, set reminders or use a moon-tracking app to help. Many apps give ritual ideas or notifications, so you can plan or be spontaneous. If you're not ready for a ritual on the exact day, wait until you are. The main idea is to use the moon's cycles as a regular reminder to pause and reflect, not as a strict schedule.

Creative Integration

Make your connection to the moon personal with small creative touches. Change items on your altar to match the moon's phase, like a dark stone for a new moon or something shiny for a full moon. Use colored paper or objects: black for new, white for full, silver for waxing, and blue for waning to represent each phase. Create moon-themed playlists to set the mood, listening to songs about new beginnings or letting go while you work or relax. Try small art projects, like drawing a crescent moon in your journal, doodling in your notes, or changing your phone background to match the moon's phases.

Journaling and Self-awareness

Use the moon's phases as inspiration for journaling. After each cycle, think about any patterns in your mood, energy, or habits. Which phases made you feel energetic or restful? Did the same challenges or breakthroughs happen again? Over time, you'll see trends, maybe you feel inspired during the waxing moon or want to rest during the waning phase. This helps you work with your natural rhythms instead of forcing a pace that doesn't suit you.

Urban and Adaptable Rituals

Living in a city means you might need to adapt. Even if you can't see the moon because of clouds or buildings, you can still connect by using an app or noticing how you feel each month. Try indoor rituals, like lighting a candle in your kitchen, or use simple substitutes like a flashlight or a cup of water to reflect on your intentions while traveling. What matters most is your focused attention, not how the ritual looks.

Using lunar cycles can help you feel grounded and bring rhythm to busy or chaotic times. Even taking a moment once a month to reflect on changes or successes can help you feel steady. The moon shows us that growth, fullness, and letting go are ongoing cycles, not something to rush. This way, you can balance ambition and rest, no matter how busy life is or how far you feel from nature.

Creating Your Own "Choose-Your-Own-Practice" Ritual Blueprint

Creating a ritual that genuinely feels like your own, not just copied from a book, can be very satisfying. It's like cooking without a recipe: you know what you like, and you mix things in a way that works for you. Rituals can be the same if you break them into basic parts and put them together to fit your mood, space, and day. Modular rituals, where you pick from a menu of core parts, help you stay creative and flexible. The main ingredients are intention, grounding, a symbolic action, maybe an offering, a clear ending, and a moment to reflect. You can mix, skip, or combine these as you like.

Let's go over what each building block means. Intention is your "why," the purpose, hope, or feeling you want to bring in. Grounding helps you feel present, not just on autopilot; this could be a breath, a favorite stretch, or pressing your feet into the floor until you feel steady. Symbolic action is where the magic happens: maybe you light a candle, tie a string, or write something down and put it away. An offering doesn't have to be big. You could pour out a little water as a gesture of gratitude or set aside a small snack as a token of thanks. Closure marks the end, like blowing out a candle, saying "done," or shaking out your hands. Reflection is pausing to notice what changed. Did you feel relief, clarity, or just a lighter mood?

To build a ritual that fits your life, pick one thing from each building block. If you have three minutes, you might set an intention like "I want calm," ground yourself with deep breaths, light a match and watch it burn out (symbolic action), say thanks (offering), blow out the match (closure), and then check in with how you feel (reflection). If you have more time or privacy, like ten minutes, you can add music, write in a journal, or include movement like gentle stretching. For group rituals, let each person add an intention or gesture; maybe everyone brings a small object for the symbolic part and shares a word at the end before reflecting together.

Making your ritual your own makes it feel real. Use words that sound like you, not something old-fashioned. If "blessing" or "invocation" feels awkward, try words like "focus," "wish," or say what you want. Swap traditional tools for things that matter to you, use your favorite mug instead of a special cup, or a rock from a walk instead of a crystal. Change the timing to fit your day; maybe you only have five minutes, or perhaps you want twenty. The more you experiment, the more natural your ritual will feel.

As you try different things, keep track of what works for you. Maybe listening to music helps you feel grounded, but sitting in silence doesn't. Writing intentions might feel powerful one week but not the next. Use a simple page to track: write the date, which building blocks you used, how you felt before and after, and any notes about what worked or didn't. Over time, you'll see patterns that can help you adjust your rituals.

Don't worry if something doesn't work. If a ritual feels boring or forced, try changing one part, switch the symbolic action (burn something instead of burying it), use a different offering (flowers instead of food), or change how you end (clap your hands instead of blowing out a candle). Even moving to a new spot or changing the time of day can make it feel fresh.

Adjusting rituals to fit your situation is important. If you're new or don't have much privacy, use intention, grounding, and one symbolic action, a simple starter ritual you can do anywhere. If you want more depth or have time alone, add offerings and longer reflection, or include music or movement if you like. For group rituals, let everyone have a role and contribute. For online groups, share intentions in chat and do symbolic actions together on video.

Take a moment to ask yourself: how has your personal ritual plan changed since you began? Are there parts that consistently work for you? Which ones have faded or changed? Think about these changes; they show your practice is growing and fits your needs.

As we finish this chapter, remember that building rituals is about being flexible and trusting yourself. You don't have to follow anyone else's rules; you can choose and change things as your life changes. In the next chapter, we'll explore symbolism and archetypes to add deeper meaning to your rituals so that you can bring your own stories into every magical act.

Chapter Six

Symbols, Archetypes, and Personal Meaning-Making

A Comparative Decoder Wheel for Archetypes Across Traditions

Have you ever noticed certain characters or patterns that keep showing up in stories, movies, or even your own life? Maybe you see the wise old mentor in both a fantasy novel and a favorite childhood teacher. You might also recognize the troublemaker, the caring parent, or the mysterious outsider among your friends or on social media. These are archetypes, which are universal patterns that appear in myths, psychology, and our personal stories.

Archetypes are universal symbols or roles in myths and stories. Jung described them as built-in images in our minds, like the Magician, Fool, Warrior, or Healer. In magical practices, these living symbols help you connect with different instincts and energies, influencing your reactions, dreams, and preferences.

Archetypes bridge your inner and outer worlds. For example, "The Mother" can manifest as the Empress in Tarot, mythic figures like Demeter or Gaia, or as your own caring impulse. The "Trickster" appears in many cultures as Loki, Coyote, or Bugs Bunny, and in Tarot as The Fool or The Magician, representing chaos and transformation.

The Shadow archetype comprises the hidden, denied, and repressed aspects of yourself: unacknowledged fears, flaws, or secret desires. Jung described confrontation with the Shadow as essential for personal growth. In myths, the Shadow takes form as adversaries or trials—embodying neglected facets that require attention, rather than evil. If you notice repeated conflicts or strong reactions, your Shadow may be influencing you.

To understand how archetypes connect across different traditions, picture using a decoder wheel, like a circular, spinning tool you may have used as a child to match letters or symbols and reveal secret codes. With this tool, you can align archetypes from one tradition to find their counterparts in another, helping you "translate" the Trickster or the Hero across different stories or belief systems. This approach makes it easier to see universal patterns beneath cultural differences.

The Trickster: Fool/Magician (Tarot), Loki (Norse), Coyote (Native American), Hermes (Greek), Anansi (West African)

The Shadow: Devil card (Tarot), Set (Egyptian), dragons/demons (myth), Jung's Shadow

The Hero: Strength card (Tarot), Hercules (Greek), King Arthur, "The Warrior" (psychology)

The Sage: Hermit (Tarot), Merlin, Odin, "Wise Elder."

These roles often overlap or shift. For instance, a Hero in one context may become an Outcast in another. Because archetypes are flexible, you can see them anywhere, in stories, media, or dreams, where familiar figures take on symbolic roles.

Why is this important for your personal or magical practice? Recognizing archetypes gives you shortcuts; you don't have to invent everything from scratch. These old patterns are there to support and inspire you. Rituals that use archetypes, like lighting a candle for Strength or journaling with The Fool, can help you bring out needed qualities. Archetypes also act as mirrors: noticing which ones appear can teach you about yourself.

Archetype Discovery Lab

Take out a notebook or open a blank document, and clearly write down a current life question or challenge you are facing. Next, think: Which archetype does this situation remind you of? For example, if your challenge is about caring for someone, think about The Mother; if you are feeling afraid, consider The Shadow; if you need to invite playfulness or mischief, look at The Trickster. Write down the archetype that comes to mind. Finally, note any immediate thoughts or feelings that arise. This step-by-step process will help you connect your current situation to universal patterns.

If you prefer to work visually, gather images that give you a strong feeling or seem important to you. These could be faces, scenes, colors, or symbols. Arrange your pictures into a collage. Once you finish, look over your collage and write down any patterns, themes, or feelings you notice. For example, if you see a lot of bright reds, you might connect this with The Warrior, while soft greens could suggest The Healer. Notice which colors or images repeat; that shows you which archetypes are most active in your life at the moment.

Watch for these archetype patterns in your daily life. Notice if a character in your favorite show acts like The Sage, or if someone at work takes on the Trickster role. By spotting these archetypes in everyday situations, you can keep practicing self-reflection. Remember, archetypes can change over time. The more you work with them, the more you'll learn about your own journey and what inspires you.

Design Personal Symbols for Sigils and Creative Correspondences

Symbols are the language of the subconscious, and magic often depends on their power. Many modern practitioners like using sigils, small, personal symbols that act as shortcuts between your intention and reality. Sigil magic, which derives from late twentieth-century chaos magic, emphasizes personal meaning over tradition. Instead of using old symbols, chaos magicians create new ones for each goal, making a direct link between the wish and the symbol. While traditional magic uses things like Mars for courage or cinnamon for passion, chaos magic-style sigils are all about making magic personal to you.

A sigil is basically a wish turned into a symbol. The process is simple but powerful: start with a clear, positive statement in the present tense, like "I am confident" or "My home feels safe." Write it down, remove any repeated letters, and you can also take out the vowels if you want. This leaves you with a string like "IMCNFDT" for "I am confident." Then, combine and shape these letters into an abstract design. Let yourself play with curves, angles, and spirals until the original words are hidden. If it feels more like doodling than drawing a perfect symbol, you're on the right track.

Charging your sigil is what gives it power. Focus your energy and imagine your wish as if it has already come true. You could look at your sigil by candlelight, breathe on it, let it sit in the sun, dance with it in your hand, or draw it on your skin to transfer energy through touch. The exact ritual you choose is less important than the intention you put into it.

Next comes activation: trust that the symbol will work and let go of the outcome. Some people destroy their sigil after charging it to release its energy; others keep it visible or integrate it into daily items. The key is to let go and allow the symbol to work.

Personal creative associations make magic more meaningful. While tradition links rose quartz with love or lavender with peace, your experiences matter more. Use objects, colors, or scents that hold personal meaning, even if they seem unusual.

Make your own correspondence table: write down intentions like "joy" or "strength," and then list the colors, smells, objects, or sounds that truly make you feel that way. Even unusual connections are fine. Over time, you'll notice unique patterns appear, like your own magical fingerprint.

Be flexible with personal symbols and associations, as their meanings can change as your life changes. Magic works best when it feels real and alive, so update your correspondence list with the seasons or during significant life changes.

For regular use, subtly incorporate your personal sigil into daily routines: draw it on your mug with a marker, sketch it on your mirror with lipstick or soap, make digital art for your phone or social media. No one needs to know the meaning but you. This keeps your intention present throughout your day.

You can mix these steps: set your intention at night, make your sigil in the morning, charge it with movement or music, and then keep it nearby for a week. Every time you see or touch it, remember what it means to you.

In the end, personal symbols and associations not only strengthen your self-trust and magical practice but also empower you to shape your experiences in meaningful ways. By weaving memories, intuition, and personal meaning into your rituals, you craft a practice that grows with you and supports your journey—making each step uniquely your own.

The Art of Meaning in Journaling and Visualization for Symbol Discovery

You likely encounter symbols daily, even if you don't realize it. A feather on your path, a clock striking oddly, graffiti tags, they may stick with you for a reason. Regular journaling helps you explore the meanings of these symbols. Start simply with a notebook or your phone's notes app. When something stands out, a symbol, object, or shape you can't forget, pause and jot down the details. Where did you see it? What was happening? How did it make you feel? Sometimes the meaning is clear, but often it isn't at first.

Writing about symbols isn't about finding the "right" answer or matching what books say. It's about paying attention and letting your own meaning come through. Try this: "Describe a symbol you noticed today, where, when, and what was happening?" Maybe you walk past the same red door every day and realize it makes you feel curious or safe, or a design on a friend's shirt reminds you of a dream. Write about what you see, but also include sounds, textures, and feelings. Over time, your journal will become a personal archive, and patterns will start to make sense.

Visualization can deepen this practice. Sometimes symbols show up in meditation or dreams and don't make sense right away. Instead of ignoring a symbol that keeps coming up, a key, an animal, or any shape, try exploring it with visualization. Close your eyes and picture the symbol. Imagine stepping into it or interacting with it. Notice the colors, temperature, and movement. If it's an object, imagine touching it. How does it feel? If it's an animal or person, does it do or say anything? Let yourself explore without worrying about whether it makes sense.

Afterward, write about this sensory experience in your journal. For example, if you imagine going into a spiral, is it warm or cold? Is it bright or dark? Are there sounds like wind, echoes, or music? Do any memories come up? Even small details can help you make connections to your life. The feelings you get, whether the spiral feels comforting or chaotic, can be just as important as what you think it means.

As you keep practicing, you'll notice that your understanding of symbols can change. Keeping track of these changes is helpful. Make a "symbol log" in your journal: whenever a symbol comes up again, write down the date, where you saw it, what was happening, and what you thought it meant that day. Months later, you might look back and see that a symbol, like a butterfly, used to mean change, but now it stands for calmness or even grief after a loss.

Learning to trust your own interpretation is freeing. There isn't a single symbol dictionary that works for everyone; meanings come from your own experience. For example, someone might have been afraid of snakes as a child, seeing them as dangerous. Later, during a time of healing, snakes began appearing more often. Instead of feeling afraid, they used journaling and meditation to see the snake as a sign of transformation and renewal, like shedding old habits. Now, the snake is a positive and encouraging symbol for them.

Your own meaning is valid, even if it goes against tradition or what others think. If a symbol gives you hope, even if tradition says it's a bad sign, trust your own view first. Over time, you'll build your intuition, making it easier to tell when something is meaningful to you and when it's just background noise.

Symbol Sighting

Pick a symbol from today that stood out. Note where you saw it, what was happening, and how you felt or what you thought. If nothing obvious comes to mind, scan your day for small details, a cloud's shape, a logo on a bag, or an image from a dream. Don't question its importance; record your honest impressions. Revisit this entry after a week, see if a new understanding emerges.

This practice isn't just about figuring out what signs mean. It's also about learning to trust yourself and building your own way of understanding meaning.

Interpreting Liminal Messages in Dreams, Synchronicity, and Everyday Omens

Liminality is the "in-between," not quite here or there. It's the quiet before sleep, the pause before dawn, or a stop in a doorway, thresholds where the ordinary blurs and something deeper can surface. Dreams, synchronicities, and omens often emerge in these spaces, unexpectedly catching your attention. Their power comes less from supernatural origins and more from arriving when your guard is down, and intuition is heightened. Whether it's a crow blocking your path before a stressful meeting or frequently spotting the same number, these moments often invite pause and reflection, making you wonder if the universe is sending a subtle message.

But not everything unusual has meaning. Our minds are built to find patterns, so sometimes things are just random. Still, there are a few ways to tell which moments might be important and that are worth noting:

Emotional Response: A bodily reaction (like goosebumps or a racing heart) is a signal for deeper significance.

Timing: Events that coincide with critical junctures or major choices can be especially relevant.

Context: Signs that appear in direct connection to your current worries or questions generally hold more weight.

Ask yourself, "What pattern keeps popping up in unexpected places?" A quick and emotional answer usually signals. Keeping track of liminal moments helps you notice repeating patterns. For dreams, keep a notebook or your phone close by so you can write down details, feelings, symbols, and key scenes right after you wake up. Note the date, main characters, setting, and any lingering emotions or questions. For coincidences and omens, make a simple log with four columns: Date, Event or Sign, What Was Happening in My Life, and Possible Meaning. For example: "4/22 – Three hawks circling – stuck at work – need bigger perspective?" Look back at your notes over the past weeks or months to identify recurring themes. This isn't about proving magic, but about making your personal meaning clearer.

Dreams are classic examples of liminal messages. Even if they don't make sense, they often reflect real emotions, hopes, and worries that are just below the surface. If you dream about losing keys before a significant change, or running through endless halls when you're stressed, think about whether these images match your feelings in real life. Some dreams are more vivid or stick with you longer; these are worth extra attention. Write down or draw the parts that repeat; sometimes your body understands their meaning before your mind does.

Synchronicity, or meaningful coincidence, often feels magical. You think of a friend, and she calls. Song lyrics answer a question you haven't said out loud. A book opens to the advice you need. These moments are easy to brush off, but when they occur around big decisions, many people feel there's something more at play. Even people who are skeptical admit that synchronicity can help you notice issues or opportunities you might have missed.

Omens can be minor or dramatic. Maybe a fox crosses your path on exam day, you run into someone from your past, or something breaks during a tense moment. Don't just write down what happened, think about how you felt right away. Did it make you do something, or snap you out of your routine? Omens often act as wake-up calls, encouraging you to pay more attention or try a new approach.

There are some pitfalls to watch out for. Confirmation bias can make you see meaning everywhere ("Owls mean change!") once you focus on a symbol, even if it's just a coincidence. Some people get obsessed, looking for messages in everything and losing touch with reality. Magical thinking can turn into escapism if you start to believe every coincidence is a sign or that the universe controls every detail of your life.

To balance intuition and skepticism, try this: when you notice a "sign," act on it once, especially if it's low risk, and then write down what happens.

Did it give you insight, relief, confusion, or change your mood? Sometimes acting on omens brings clarity. Other times, it shows that not every sign is a message you need to follow.

It takes practice to develop this mindset, but it helps you move through life with both curiosity and good judgment. Trust yourself to notice what really matters and let the rest go. Liminal messages are meant to encourage deeper awareness, not to give strict instructions.

A Personalization Playbook for Building Your Own Symbolic Language

Building your own symbolic language is a creative, practical way to keep your practice personal and adaptable. Every day, you likely notice images, objects, or gestures that subtly capture your attention. These can become the foundation of a meaningful personal system that resonates more deeply than any ancient script. Start by collecting symbols that feel significant: a recurring natural pattern, a phrase that sticks in your mind, or a shape doodled during meetings. To organize your collection, start a "Book of Symbols." This could be a journal, a binder with sketches or magazine clippings, or a digital folder with photos, voice notes, and scanned drawings. Don't worry about making it perfect; what matters is that it's real and personal. Give each symbol its own page or file. Write down where you found it, what it meant to you at the time, and any feelings it brought up. Over time, your book will show how your inner world changes. If you like digital tools, use note-taking apps or digital scrapbooks to save meaningful moments, take photos of graffiti, street signs, or interesting objects, and add notes about your feelings and what was happening.

Remember, symbols can change over time. What a blackbird means to you one month might change after a tough conversation or a big event. It helps to review your symbols regularly. Each month, look through your symbol collection and ask yourself, "Has any meaning changed?" For example, a gold ring might go from comforting to bitter after a breakup, or an old photo might shift from nostalgia to a sign of resilience. Let these changes happen and be honest with yourself, meanings are supposed to evolve.

Sharing your symbols with others can help you see things in new ways. Meet with a friend or a small group to discuss your symbols. You'll notice that the same image might mean hope to you, but feel like a challenge to someone else. These conversations deepen your understanding and offer new ideas, even when you don't always agree.

Bring your symbols into everyday life through creative expression. Draw, paint, or sculpt them, even if you don't consider yourself artistic. Wear your symbol as jewelry, stitch it onto clothing, or carve it into candles. Arrange meaningful objects on your altar, a shell from a trip or a pebble from a tough day. If you like crafts, turn a symbol into a keychain or patch for your bag. The more visible these symbols are, the stronger their connection to your intentions and feelings.

Combine traditional symbols with your own meanings for more depth. For example, you might use a rose for love and pair it with a family heirloom, such as a small spoon, to connect your heritage to your rituals. These combinations bring together shared wisdom and your personal story. When setting up your altar or rituals, try using one traditional symbol and one personal one, and see how they work together.

Welcoming new symbols is worth celebrating. Hold a simple yearly "symbol ceremony": light a candle, arrange your new symbols, and say out loud what each one means to you now. Thank them for how they've shaped your experience, and ask for guidance as their meanings change over time.

Symbol Curation

This week, take fifteen minutes to look over your symbol collection, whether it's on paper, digital, or just items on your desk. Which symbol feels most important right now? Which one feels less meaningful? If you notice a change, write down why. Are there new images or objects that stand out to you? Make room for them, add them to your book, wear them, or put them on your altar.

This way, your practice stays flexible and truly personal. You don't have to follow someone else's old rules; you're creating a symbolic language that changes and grows with you over time. As you finish this chapter, remember: symbols aren't mere decoration; they connect intention, memory, and imagination. Your evolving symbolic language will keep your practice relevant and alive. Next, we'll explore how mindfulness and self-reflection can ground these creative practices in daily life, making the ordinary quietly enchanted.

Chapter Seven

Mindfulness, Self-Reflection, and Shadow Work

Guided Journaling to Transform Experience into Wisdom

Mindfulness and self-reflection are powerful tools for personal growth, transforming fleeting experiences into lasting wisdom by grounding insights in everyday actions. Journaling is essential in this integration process. Rather than simply noting events, journaling helps you fuse mystical moments with daily life, deepening your understanding and aiding retention. Writing also clarifies recurring patterns or contradictions, ensuring the wisdom from magical moments becomes part of your routine.

Journaling after magical practice lets you look closely at your experience and value it. When you write about a ritual, small details come to light, like candlelight, how your body felt, or a certain smell. What stood out to you? Did you feel tense, calm, distracted, or focused? Did any worries pop up? These details offer clues about your process and what you need.

Sometimes, writing connects experiences in surprising ways. For example, meditation might bring up old memories, or bedtime rituals could help you sleep better. Journaling helps you blend magic into your daily life.

You don't have to write perfectly. If complete sentences feel awkward, try making mind maps by drawing circles for emotions and lines for connections. You can sketch your altar or how the energy felt. Try writing a conversation between parts of yourself, like "Doubt" and "Curiosity." Use bullet points for quick notes, such as "tingling hands," "surprised by tears," or "thought of my sister." If you like, write poetry and let your feelings shape your words. You can even make a collage with pieces of your day, like leaves or paper scraps. The main goal is to be honest and go deep, not to be neat.

Journaling can sometimes bring up discomfort or old pain, so handle intense topics gently. If a page feels heavy, close your journal with care: press your hand to the page, take a breath, and picture the feelings settling into the paper. Some people seal difficult entries with wax or use a special bookmark to mark them as finished. You can write an affirmation like "I am safe" or "This stays here." If you're worried about privacy, create your own shorthand, use symbols only you know, write in another language, or make up abbreviations. Keep your journals in a safe place, encrypt digital ones, or burn pages that feel too sensitive to keep.

Guided prompts can help you go deeper when you're stuck or want more than surface reflection. Consider these:

"Describe a recent ritual. What did you sense, feel, or notice?"

"When did you last feel connected to something bigger?" This might be during meditation, listening to music, or laughing with friends.

"What recurring themes or symbols appear in your life?" Maybe certain animals or words keep cropping up.

"What fear or resistance surfaced during your last magical practice?" Naming blocks can make them less intimidating and offer space to work through them.

Creative Journaling Menu

Mind map: Draw nodes for emotions and link them to experiences.
Sketch: Illustrate an image or symbol from your ritual.
Dialogue: Write a conversation between two inner voices.
Bullet list: Jot down quick sensory impressions.
Short poem: Capture a mood or insight in a few lines.
Collage: Glue found materials related to your experience.
Coded entry: Use personal shorthand for privacy.
Ritual closure: End with a wax drip, breath, affirmation, or hand over the page.

Journaling creates space for self-discovery without outside approval, and it keeps you learning from your insights, making you more aware and helping you notice even small changes. This way, moments of wisdom become part of daily life instead of getting lost in the busyness. Just as journaling integrates experiences, shadow work takes you even deeper, addressing aspects of yourself that may not surface in day-to-day reflection.

Shadow Work for the Modern Mystic Using Tools for Integration

Shadow work is a practice for personal growth and wholeness that involves getting to know and accepting the hidden or neglected parts of yourself. While the term "shadow work" might sound dark or scary, it is a helpful practice found in both magical and psychological traditions. It's about exploring the parts of yourself you usually keep hidden, not to judge them, but to shine a light on emotions, habits, or stories you'd rather avoid. These parts aren't "bad"; they just haven't been noticed. The goal is to make room for your whole self, including your imperfections.

You don't need to face your biggest fears right away. Begin with simple tools. Ask yourself, "What trait in others annoys me most? Could that be in me, too?" Often, the things we dislike in others show us hidden parts of ourselves. Maybe arrogance in others bothers you, or you notice envy. Seeing these patterns isn't about blaming yourself; it's about honestly noticing what's there.

Mirror work can be a strong, though sometimes awkward, way to begin. Stand in front of a mirror, look yourself in the eye, and speak kindly to the parts you usually hide. You might say, "I see you, even when you're scared." Let any feelings come up, discomfort, tears, or relief. Even a minute or two can help you judge yourself less and be kinder to your hidden parts.

Archetype mapping is another helpful tool. Write down roles or qualities you push aside, like "the troublemaker," "the needy one," or "the skeptic." Notice where they show up in your life and what positive qualities, if any, they might offer. Sometimes, what feels burdensome is actually protective or highlights an unmet need; your "exiled" selves may only want acknowledgment.

Shadow work can also be done as a ritual. Sit quietly with a lit candle and focus on its flame. Let difficult feelings or memories come up naturally, without trying to force them. Imagine the candle's light slowly shining on emotions or stories you've hidden. Don't try to analyze, notice any images, words, or feelings that come up. If something heavy appears, thank it for showing up and remind yourself you can come back to it later.

For deeper release and healing, try a simple ceremony. Write down a limiting belief or story, such as "I must please everyone" or "I fear being seen." Fold the paper and sit with it for a moment. Then, you can safely burn it, bury it, or put it under a stone to show you're open to change. Afterward, say an affirmation like "I welcome all parts of myself." You might also make a "shadow altar," a special place with objects like dark stones for strength or feathers for lightness, to honor growth through honesty instead of struggle.

Shadow work often stirs intense feelings. Shadow work can bring up strong feelings, so self-care is important. Before you go deep, plan what will support you, people you can talk to, grounding activities like having tea, taking walks, or spending time with pets and friends. Keep your support list somewhere you can see it, like on a sticky note or with comfort items nearby. If you notice ongoing anxiety, mood swings, or overwhelming memories, take a break and reach out for professional help. A trained therapist can help you work through these feelings safely. What supports me when I face my shadow?" It might be a nonjudgmental friend, soothing music, pets, or spiritual practices that ground you. Name and draw strength from these as you do shadow work.

Shadow work can make you feel vulnerable, but it also brings real freedom. Every kind step you take, like journaling about irritations, saying affirmations in the mirror, mapping hidden parts of yourself, meditating with a candle, or creating supportive rituals, helps you bring your discoveries into daily life. By working with your shadow, you become more authentic and energized, supporting both your personal magic and your growth. Building on these insights, you may wish to explore even further with practices like meditative pathworking, which guides you deeper into your inner landscape.

Explore Inner Landscapes with Meditative Pathworking

Meditative pathworking is a creative tool for self-insight and guidance. It helps you explore your inner world to find answers that might not be immediately obvious. Pathworking uses your imagination, curiosity, and trust in your own process. Unlike guided meditation, where you follow someone else's voice, pathworking lets you be the explorer and storyteller. You don't just picture a peaceful place or focus on your breath; you enter symbolic spaces that hold meaning for you. These might be gardens, labyrinths, temples, or other landscapes that exist only in your mind but feel real as you imagine them. Pathworking is different from regular visualization because you interact with what you find, ask questions, get messages, and meet guides or animals that show up unexpectedly.

To begin, find a comfortable spot where you won't be interrupted. Close your eyes and take a few slow breaths. It helps to set a gentle intention, maybe clarity, healing, or just curiosity. Now, picture yourself standing at the entrance to a lush, walled garden. The gate opens as you approach. Step inside. What do you notice first? Are there flowers in bloom, or is it wild and tangled? Is the air warm or cool? As you move deeper, pay attention to one plant that catches your eye. Approach it. Notice its color, shape, and scent. Does it remind you of something or someone? Maybe an animal shows up, a bird, a fox, or something less familiar. Ask if it has a message or enjoy its company. Sometimes a guide appears, human or otherwise. Listen to see if they offer advice or a question. Another pathworking idea is to imagine yourself at the entrance of a winding stone labyrinth. Each turn stands for a challenge or question you're dealing with right now. As you walk, notice any feelings that come up: frustration, hope, or confusion. When you reach the center, you might find a gift waiting for you, like a glowing stone, a key, or a word whispered in the air. As you leave, think about what burden you want to let go of. Imagine it falling away with each step back to the exit. This is a way to let go of what you no longer need and welcome something new into your life.

For a different experience, try entering the Elemental Temple. Imagine four doorways, each marked with a symbol for earth, air, fire, or water. Choose the one that feels right to you today. If you pick earth, you might find yourself in a cave with crystals and roots, touch the walls, and feel their strength. If you pick air, maybe a breeze lifts you into the clouds, where you can watch your thoughts drift by and listen for inspiration. Fire might bring you warmth and courage, while water could invite feelings and reflection. Each element offers its own lessons and gifts, depending on what you need right now.

When you feel finished, or your mind starts to wander, gently return to your normal awareness. Don't rush to figure everything out; let your impressions settle first. Later, write down or sketch what you saw, heard, or felt. Ask yourself questions like: What stood out? Did any symbols repeat? Were there words or feelings that stayed with you? You can turn your notes into images or make a "pathworking map," a visual collage showing the places and beings you encountered.

It's normal to run into problems during pathworking. Sometimes your mind races with random thoughts, or nothing comes to mind at all. This doesn't mean you're doing it wrong; it just means your mind is busy or needs time to get used to this kind of practice. If you feel restless, pause and focus on your breath for a minute before trying again. Saying out loud what you hope will happen, like "I want to meet an animal guide" or "I want to find water," can help things move forward. Other times, just noticing your distraction, like saying, "My brain is busy tonight," can help you gently return to your path.

You don't have to force anything. If you can't see clear images, focus on feelings, sounds, or even imagined textures and temperatures. Your subconscious communicates in many ways, not just with pictures. With practice and patience, these inner worlds will become richer and easier to explore. Each time you visit, you may find new insights or surprises, sometimes what seems like fantasy reveals truths you wouldn't have found by thinking alone.

Pathworking can be a powerful way to work through emotional blocks or to gain clarity about decisions. Each time you do it, whether for a short or a long session, you build a better connection with your inner world, a place where wisdom awaits you.

Progress Trackers to Measure Spiritual Growth with Compassion

It's natural to wonder if your magical or mystical practices are "working" or if you're making progress. However, spiritual growth rarely happens in a straight line; progress is cyclical and nonlinear, like the moon's phases or changing seasons. The urge to compare yourself to others can twist your experience into a competition, but your path is uniquely yours, with its own rhythm.

Building Personal Progress Trackers

Tracking your progress can help you notice subtle shifts and stay present without demanding perfection. A simple way is a monthly "state of the spirit" review. Keep it low-pressure: note your mood, energy, and sense of connection, and which practices were supportive or felt stale. Record questions, insights, or patterns honestly and without judgment. Over time, these notes will highlight trends, perhaps you feel more confident after regular meditation, or that certain rituals no longer serve you. After rituals, try a "before and after" check-in. Rate your comfort, confidence, and curiosity on a 1–5 scale both before and after a practice. Notice if the numbers shift or if you feel more open or relaxed. These scales aren't for grading yourself; they're a way to notice change, even subtle boosts in confidence.

Milestone Moments

Don't focus solely on big achievements, such as complex rituals or visionary experiences. Small wins are just as essential as trusting your intuition, admitting you need rest, or maintaining a grounding practice for a week. Keep a visible "milestone moments" log, a notebook, sticky notes, or a note on your phone, where you quickly jot down any moment that feels like growth: "Spoke my intention out loud," "Tried something new," "Noticed a pattern and paused." This shifts your focus to what's developing rather than what's missing.

Celebrating Progress

Celebrate milestones and meaningfully. Light a candle for each milestone you achieve, or add a stone to a jar for every week you show up. These symbols make your effort tangible and help you see you're moving forward, even if slowly or imperfectly. Try a short monthly ritual: gather your milestone notes, read them aloud, and thank yourself for your effort, celebrating both successes and lessons from setbacks.

Creative and Digital Trackers

If you enjoy creativity, try visual trackers like progress mandalas, draw a circle, split it into segments for confidence, self-kindness, courage, etc., and color them as you notice growth. You could also use mood or color wheels, shading each day according to your emotional state to reveal trends over time. Vision boards with words, images, or symbols help focus your intentions and track qualities you want to grow.

For digital tracking, use habit-tracking apps to log daily practices, meditation, spellwork, or to remember to pause and breathe. At week's or month's end, review your streaks, celebrating consistency rather than perfection. These tools can help you notice both periods of dedication and times of neglect, without feeding into guilt.

Compassionate Reflection

Remember: tracking isn't about proving you're better than yesterday or anyone else. It's about clarity, kindness, and honoring your effort. Growth isn't about always feeling great; sometimes it's just about persisting through boredom or doubt. Regularly ask yourself: "What am I proud of this month?" Notice even tiny shifts, a kinder inner voice, the willingness to try again after frustration, a moment of peace amid chaos.

If you want to weave ritual into this, dedicate a monthly celebration to your progress. Light a candle, review your trackers, and acknowledge at least one thing about your resilience, even if it's just "I tried." If you like physical symbols, add a bead or stone to a jar each month; over time, it becomes a visual testament to your ongoing dedication.

Embracing the Cyclical Nature of Growth

Every cycle of practice has its own pace, sometimes slow, sometimes unpredictable. Compassionate tracking means staying curious, not judgmental, and honoring effort instead of chasing perfection. Growth comes in waves, stumbles, and unexpected leaps, a rhythm uniquely yours and worth celebrating every step of the way.

Embracing Skepticism as a Spiritual Strength

Uncertainty has a way of creeping in at the oddest times. Maybe it shows up when you're sitting on the floor in the middle of a ritual, suddenly thinking, "Am I just playing pretend?" Or you catch yourself questioning if anything you just did matters at all. This isn't a sign of failure or weakness; it's living, breathing curiosity. In fact, doubt has always been a traveling companion for mystics and magicians; history is full of seekers who questioned their own visions, asked too many questions for comfort, and still found deep meaning. Take Teresa of Ávila, who confessed to spiritual dryness and confusion as often as ecstasy, or Aleister Crowley, infamous for flipping between wild belief and biting skepticism. Even the philosopher Socrates, not exactly a magician, built his life's work on "not knowing," treating questions as more valuable than answers. These figures didn't push away their doubts; they dug into them, letting uncertainty crack open new insights.

Living with ambiguity isn't just tolerable; it's powerful. Instead of running from the unknown, try sitting with it. Pull up a chair for your questions, "What if nothing happens? What if I'm wrong?" and let them hang in the air. You can practice this with what I call "maybe meditation." Just sit quietly with a question in mind, no need to solve it, and notice what comes up. Maybe your chest tightens, maybe your mind races, or maybe it goes blank. Gently notice these sensations without rushing to explain or fix them. You might discover that holding a question, rather than demanding an answer, feels oddly freeing. If you want to take this further, sketch or collage your idea of "the unknown." What colors, shapes, or images come up? Is it foggy or clear, scary or inviting? Sometimes giving form to uncertainty makes it feel less threatening.

If you're not sure where to start, try this: Ask yourself, "What am I unsure about right now?" Maybe it's whether a spell worked, or if meditation really changes anything. Where do you feel that not-knowing in your body? Is it a knot in your stomach, a flutter in your hands? Put words or drawings to these sensations; you might find the act of naming transforms them. This is not about forcing certainty but befriending your own questions.

Experimentation becomes a lifeline when nothing feels certain. Treat magical practice as a series of experiments rather than tests you must pass. Keep an "experiment log" where you jot down what you tried, maybe a new ritual or meditation, and what actually happened. Did you feel calmer? Did nothing happen at all? Both are valuable data. When something flops, ask yourself: "What did I learn from this so-called failure?" Maybe you noticed that candle magic fits better in the morning than at night, or that chanting makes you uncomfortable but drawing sigils feels right. Over time, these experiments add up; you'll build a practice grounded in honest experience instead of borrowed rules.

Holding beliefs lightly takes courage and flexibility. It's easy to get stuck thinking there's only one right way to believe, or feeling shame when your experience doesn't match someone else's story. But compassionate skepticism means allowing yourself to revise, adapt, or even discard what no longer fits. Repeat this affirmation when you feel lost: "It's okay not to know, mystery is part of the magic." One practitioner I know spent years jumping from tradition to tradition, doubting every technique until they realized the questioning itself was shaping their path. Their practice grew richer once they stopped demanding certainty and started playing with possibilities.

If you're hungry for more on spiritual agnosticism and critical inquiry, there's plenty out there. Authors like Alan Watts explore not-knowing as wisdom rather than weakness, while Sharon Salzberg writes beautifully about faith as an open-ended process rather than a closed system. Treat books and teachings as invitations to test ideas, not as instruction manuals written in stone.

Mysticism thrives in uncertainty, the gaps between what you think you know and what you're still discovering. Doubt isn't just allowed; it's welcomed as fuel for deeper exploration. When you treat skepticism as an asset, not an enemy, you open yourself to new ways of practicing and understanding magic that feel alive, personal, and resilient.

Recommended Reading

Alan Watts – *The Wisdom of Insecurity*

Sharon Salzberg – *Faith: Trusting Your Own Deep Experience*

Mark Vernon – *How to Be an Agnostic*

Wrapping up this chapter, remember that every step, whether full of clarity or clouded by doubt, contributes to your lived experience of magic and mysticism. Sitting with uncertainty means honoring both questions and answers as sources of wisdom. As we continue forward, keep this spaciousness alive; the next chapter will show how creativity and aesthetics can further nourish your magical practice, making space for beauty and delight alongside inquiry.

Chapter Eight

Art, Music, and the Sensory Experience of Magic

Creating Beauty as a Channel for Spirit with Sacred Spaces Art

Have you ever moved things around on your desk or coffee table to make the space feel right, even if you're not sure why? Maybe you arrange a special stone, a photo, or a small clay figure until something inside you feels balanced. This isn't just cleaning up, it's a quiet kind of magic. Think of your altar, or any special spot, as both a sacred space and a living piece of art. Like a painting, its arrangement is a personal expression: a way to connect with your spirit and focus. It's not about copying someone else's idea of an altar. It's about creating beauty that brings intention and inspiration into your space, turning any surface into a vessel for your own energy, just as an artist shapes a blank canvas.

The way things look really does affect your mood and focus. When you arrange your altar with care, it does more than look nice; it changes how you feel in the space. The way you place objects, choose colors, and decide on the layout, whether neat or freer, shapes the atmosphere and your mindset. Making an altar is more like creating a painting or sculpture using objects, colors, and memories rather than building a distant shrine. Each time you change it, you adjust the energy, sometimes making it brighter, calmer, or more focused on a wish or need. Your altar evolves as a dynamic art piece reflecting your inner world and speaking through its arrangement and beauty.

Add your own creative touch; artistic skill isn't needed. Paint a blue background for peace, draw meaningful symbols, sculpt with clay, or fold origami cranes for hope. Any art form, like watercolor or digital art, brings your altar to life. Handmade items are special because they carry your intention. You can use family keepsakes to connect memory and spirit, blending past and present. Simple shapes or patterns on paper or stone help set intentions for harmony.

Color isn't just for artists; it's important in magic and altar design, too. Every color has its own energy, even if you don't notice it. Choose colors that match your intention: orange or gold for courage, green or blue for healing, white or yellow for clarity. You can arrange candles, stones, or fabrics from dark to light to create a sense of movement and change. There are no strict rules, so trust what feels right. If you're not sure where to begin, try using colors that match the season or your ritual's purpose, like red for winter's passion or pink for spring renewal.

Let your altar change as your needs and moods change. Let it reflect your own transitions and what's happening in the world around you. In spring, you might use fresh flowers; in autumn, leaves or acorns; in winter, crystals or white stones. You can also make altars for certain feelings, use soft fabrics and comforting items for grief, bright or playful things for joy, or just a candle and one symbol for new beginnings. If you have little space or are traveling, make a small altar in a tin or pouch with a cloth, a photo, a bead, or a pebble. This way, you can create a sacred space anywhere, even in a hotel, outside, or in a car.

Sacred space doesn't have to be something you do alone. Children's art can add fresh, spontaneous energy. Work with friends or family, paint rocks together for shared wishes, or make a group collage to celebrate a season or event. Let these creations stay as long as they feel right. Every new piece changes the energy, sometimes making it lively, sometimes gentle, but always full of life.

Designing Your Living Altar

Take a moment to stand in front of your altar or any meaningful surface. Clear everything off and take three slow breaths, paying attention to how the empty space feels. Slowly add objects back, starting with what feels most important to you right now. Don't stress about making it symmetrical or following tradition; arrange things by color, size, or memory, whatever feels right. After each item, notice how the space feels: is it lighter, more focused, or more open? Keep moving things until the arrangement feels balanced or has the energy you want.

When you're done, write about the process. Notice which items you wanted to put back first, which ones stayed, and what these choices say about your needs or how you're feeling. Use what you learn to spot changing priorities or patterns. Try this exercise again when the seasons change, after big events, or whenever your energy feels stuck.

Remember, making an altar is about creating beauty for your spirit and grounding your intentions. When your art and objects feel right for you, magic becomes visible and present in your space.

Use Music and Voice in Ritual for Sacred Soundscapes

Sound works quietly, changing your mood and energy before you even notice. Whether it's music at a concert or humming in your kitchen, sound shapes the atmosphere and gets you ready for what's next. In ritual, sound is more than just background; it helps shift your awareness and set your intention. A steady rhythm, a chant, or even a simple hum can take you out of everyday life. Science shows that music changes your brainwaves and can create trance states. Fast beats give you energy, slow rhythms help you relax, and when music sweeps you away, it's because your brain is syncing with the sound.

People all over the world have used music and voice in rituals for a long time. Drumming circles, temple bells, chanting monks, and singing bowls are just a few examples. Whether it's Sufi whirling with drums, Tibetan monks chanting "Om Mani Padme Hum," or West African polyrhythms, the idea is the same: music is healing, a doorway, and a sacred language.

You don't need to be a musician to create powerful ritual soundscapes. Make playlists that match your intention: for grounding, pick slow, steady beats like drumming, cello, or folk strings. For trance or meditation, try ambient synths, drones, or repeating chants, sounds that fade into the background until you feel lighter. For celebrations, use energetic music like handclaps, world percussion, joyful pop, or anything that makes you want to move. For cleansing, try chimes, rain sounds, or recordings of birds and water to clear out old energy. Think about whether you want lyrics; words can help you focus or sometimes distract, so instrumental music often gives you more mental space.

Live sound feels even more immediate. Your voice is the most personal instrument you have, and ritual isn't about putting on a show. Humming by yourself can calm your nerves and help you connect with your body. Feel the vibrations in your chest and notice how they relax you. Try holding out vowel sounds like "ah," "ee," or "mm" at different pitches to see which ones feel best. Simple mantras, such as repeating a word like "peace" or "release," can help you stay focused. Play with volume, whispers feel close and personal, strong singing fills the space, and call-and-response can help you connect with others.

Combine your voice with movement, walk in circles while you chant, or sway as you hum. If you feel shy, try humming while you do chores to get used to it. When you're alone, experiment with being loud, playful, or gentle. In groups, try saying intentions out loud or repeating each other's words. The main idea is to experiment with voice and movement, start simple if you're nervous, and focus on how the sound feels rather than how skilled you are. Let sound help shift your awareness.

Homemade instruments add a special touch to rituals, and you don't need expensive gear. Use a pot lid or bucket as a drum. Fill a jar with beans or rice to make a simple rattle. Clapping can mark transitions and boost energy, and snapping your fingers works if you don't have much space. You can also tap sticks or pencils on a table to create grounding rhythms.

For melody, you can use metal or crystal singing bowls if you have them, or tap water glasses filled to different levels for gentle tones. Rainsticks are easy to make with a cardboard tube and some grains for a soothing sound. Hang wind chimes by a window or hold them during a ritual for a light, airy sound. Everyday items can be magical too: shells make soft clinks, keys jingle, and stones tapped together create earthy sounds.

You don't need talent; what matters is being present and open. Try new sounds to keep rituals lively. Notice which rhythms or tones shift your mood, and let sound guide your practice.

Build Your Ritual Sound Palette

Spend ten minutes before your next ritual exploring different sounds. Collect things that make noise, like kitchen tools, craft supplies, or keys, and try tapping, shaking, or even singing through them. Make a quick playlist with three songs for each mood: grounding (steady drums), trance (ambient sounds), celebration (upbeat music), and cleansing (rain or wind). Hum while you set your intentions or arrange your space. Afterward, write down which sounds changed your mood the most or felt the strongest, and keep your sound collection nearby, adding new favorites as you find them.

Sound helps you stay present and can open doors to the mystical. Whether you use a homemade drum, jingling keys, your own humming, or a song that stirs old memories, rituals come alive through sound. You don't need fancy tools or lots of training, just curiosity, attention, and a willingness to listen closely. Let music and your voice guide you deeper into your practice and help you connect in new ways. The main point: anyone can create powerful ritual soundscapes with everyday items and a little presence.

Engage All Senses in Magical Work with Scent, Texture, and Taste

Magic feels real when you experience it with your senses, not just in your mind. The smell of cinnamon and orange from a simmering pot, or the feel of cool sand in your hands, can ground you right away. Scent, touch, and taste are often missed in spiritual practice, but they're some of the fastest ways to bring you into the present. Your body remembers these sensations, smells like baking bread can bring back childhood memories, and lavender can help you relax. Scent is more than just perfume or incense; it's a direct way to change your mood and trigger memories. A single whiff can help you go from distracted to focused, or from scattered to calm.

Adding scent to your ritual helps your whole body respond. You don't need expensive oils or rare ingredients. Simple things like simmering water with orange slices, cloves, or cinnamon sticks can warm and energize your space. Making tea or warming milk with honey can gently comfort your senses. You can also use dry kitchen spices like rosemary for clarity, bay leaf for protection, or ground coffee for alertness. Rubbing scented oil on your wrists or holding a small bag of herbs can help you focus. The most important thing is your intention: pause as you breathe in, and let the scent bring a sense of the sacred.

Texture can also help ground your mind. The world is full of magical things to touch; reach out. Holding smooth stones, rough bark, or soft fabric can help settle your thoughts. Many people use special altar cloths: velvet for comfort, burlap for grounding, or silk for clarity. A bowl filled with rice, glass beads, sand, or marbles can help steady you before a ritual, giving you something to focus on. Even candles feel different, beeswax, paraffin, or soy, and using textured paper for notes or spells adds another layer to the experience.

Taste makes magic feel close and real; you actually take your intention in. Rituals don't need big meals. Drink herbal teas with purpose: chamomile for peace, peppermint for energy, or ginger for courage. Add honey for abundance or healing, and use salt for protection and grounding. Chocolate, ancient and modern, can be a special offering to yourself or to spirits. Baking bread or simple cakes becomes sacred when you do it with intention, focus on what you want as you knead the dough, and let your energy rise with the bread.

You don't need to be perfect or have special tools for these sensory experiences. Simmer pots work with any spices or citrus peels you have on hand. Dried herbs are fine if you don't have fresh ones. To layer scents, light incense as your tea steams, and notice how the scents blend. Everyday things work too, a favorite mug, a seashell, or a ribbon on your wrist. As you get ready for ritual, pay attention to how each item feels in your hand, not just how it looks.

Combining these elements makes your intention stronger. Match scents with your goals: lavender and blue cloth for calm, lemon peel and gold ribbon for clarity, cinnamon and orange for energy. Match tastes, too: drink lemon tea for clarity rituals, or eat dark chocolate before meditating to ground yourself. Change your touch bowls to fit your mood: soft rice to calm anxiety, cool stones to help you focus, or rough sand to boost motivation.

Ritual snacks and drinks can turn everyday moments into something special. Make smoothies or teas, and bless them. Stir clockwise to bring in energy, or counterclockwise to let go. If you're alone, whisper your intention. If you're with others, hold hands or cups together in silence before drinking. Sharing taste brings everyone together, even if it's just you.

Baking bread has a long history of magic. As you knead and shape the dough, focus on love, gratitude, or whatever you need most. Share the bread with friends to spread that energy. You can do the same with fruit:

carefully slice and arrange apples or pears as offerings to ancestors and deities, or to honor yourself.

Using seasonal ingredients helps you feel more connected: mulled cider in winter, strawberries in spring, and tomatoes in summer. Eating local or seasonal foods ties your practice to the rhythms of the land, even if you shop at a regular store. Just pick something that feels fresh and present.

Scent helps you remember and marks important changes; some smells can instantly remind you of people or moments. Touch keeps you steady when your thoughts are racing, and taste makes ritual something you can really experience, not just think about.

Magic is strongest when you use all your senses. Rituals become real and memorable when you can smell, touch, and taste them, not just picture them in your mind. When you involve your whole body, magic feels immediate, vivid, and real.

Personalize the Physical and the Visual with Ritual Tools

It feels good to hold something you've made or decorated yourself and sense the intention you put into it. Making your own magical tools isn't just about saving money or showing off your skills; it's about putting a part of yourself into the process. You choose what matters, what materials you like, and every mark or knot becomes personal. Making a wand, staff, or charm is a ritual in itself, a slow and thoughtful process that connects your ideas with your hands. Each step, like sanding a branch, wrapping thread, or painting a symbol, lets you focus on what you want the tool to do. Sometimes, making the tool is just as magical as using it.

You don't have to be an artist or woodworker to make your own tools. Start with something simple. Maybe you find a smooth stick on a walk, clean it, and keep it somewhere you can see it until you're ready. Wrap the handle with colored thread or ribbon for a purpose: green for growth, purple for intuition, red for confidence. Add beads for texture and color, each one chosen for a memory or wish. Glue stones or crystals to the tip to make your wand unique and boost its power. Even a thick marker or wooden spoon can become a wand with some paint or a burned-in design. For ritual knives, you can paint or wrap thrift-store butter knives, and for chalices, decorate a favorite mug or glass with paint or charms.

Don't hesitate to decorate things you already own. You can use a woodburning tool to carve symbols, runes, or words onto staffs and wands. Acrylic paints or markers can turn plain stones into powerful talismans. Pick symbols that mean something to you, or make up your own. You can carve candles with pins or toothpicks, then paint them with melted wax in different colors. Glass jars can become spell containers when you add charms, paint symbols, or tie on cloth. Wrapping handles with ribbon makes them stand out, and you can add small bells, feathers, or shells for extra energy.

You might find that old things you have, like outgrown jewelry, single earrings, or chipped cups, are ready for a new purpose. Reusing these items can add extra meaning to your practice. Thrift stores can also have hidden treasures, like a unique spoon, a favorite bowl, or a scarf that could become an altar cloth. With some imagination and maybe a few online tutorials, everyday items can become magical when you use them with intention.

Where you get your materials is important. The energy of a tool begins before you even touch it. Collect fallen branches (don't break them off living trees), look for shells after storms, or pick up stones from riverbanks to connect your tools to your local area and show respect for the land. If you use paints, glues, or finishes, choose non-toxic, eco-friendly options like water-based paints, natural oils, or beeswax polish. Don't use rare plants or buy products from endangered animals; magic that harms takes more than it gives. If you use items from thrift stores, clean them physically and energetically: wash with saltwater if it's safe, pass them through incense smoke, or hold them and imagine any old energy leaving.

Some of the most special tools are made with others. Crafting together adds meaning, and shared laughter and stories become part of every knot and brushstroke. In some groups I've worked with, we made group altar cloths by having each person sew a patch, paint a symbol, or tie on a ribbon for their hopes that season. Group candles can be carved or painted together at the start of a ritual, with each person adding a symbol or word before lighting them as a community. There's real power in creating together; everyone who helps adds something you can feel, even if you can't see it.

A friend's coven has a tradition for every full moon: they collect sticks from a favorite park and, together, decorate them into wands, sharing stories about their goals for the month. Each staff member holds not just personal intention but the care of the whole group. When someone needs extra support, everyone "charges" their staff by passing it hand to hand around the circle.

If you don't have a community right now, you can still include others in spirit. Use materials given to you by friends, like a stone from someone's garden or thread from a sibling's sewing kit, or dedicate your project to those who support you.

Whether you're painting symbols on river stones or gluing beads onto an old spoon from your grandmother's kitchen, making things changes both the object and you. Every mark you make carries intention, and even missed stitches are small blessings. Tools made this way become reminders of who you are and where you've been, always ready to help you focus your energy when you need it most.

As this chapter ends, remember that magic is about how you do things and what you include in the process. Your hands can create beauty and power from simple objects, turning them into companions for your practice. When you personalize your tools, you add your own story to every ritual, grounding your magic in your own experience and creativity instead of following someone else's rules.

Next, we'll look at how ethics and community shape a sustainable practice. Magic doesn't happen alone; it becomes stronger through intention, respect, and connecting with others and the world around you.

Chapter Nine

Ethics, Community, and Responsible Practice

Checklists for Responsible Practice Using the "Ethics First" Approach

Before beginning a new ritual or planning a gathering, always ask: "Is this right? Am I honoring the source? How might my actions impact others?" Placing ethics first means making consent, transparency, and accountability your priorities. Pause and ensure your actions align with your values and serve others mindfully.

Intentions and choices shape responsible practice. Consent requires clear information and safety for everyone involved, ask rather than assume, and accept 'no.' Transparency means open intentions and honesty about origins and limits. Accountability consists of learning from mistakes and accepting responsibility.

Humility unites these elements. Self-reflect often. Check your motives before acting. Ego might urge you to show off, or curiosity might push you too far. Being humble means admitting you don't know everything and staying open to learning.

Make ethics practical: use checklists with guiding questions before any ritual or group activity. For solo practice: Is this respectful of its sources? Have I investigated its background and openness? Am I mindful of effects, like allergies or privacy? What motivates me: service, curiosity, or ego? These questions help you spot problems early.

Group work brings added responsibilities: obtain informed consent, explain rituals openly, and respect anyone who declines or observes. Credit sources remain open to feedback and prioritize a respectful environment.

Cross-cultural practice needs extra care. Before using practices from another culture, especially marginalized ones, ask: "Have I researched the source and context? Does it require permission or initiation? Have I thanked those who preserve it?" If unsure, consider consulting community elders or cultural experts to ensure respectful engagement, helping practitioners avoid unintentional harm and fostering responsible practice.

Ethics-First Checklist

Daily Rituals:

- Have I researched the origin of this practice?

- Is it from an open tradition?

- Am I acting from respect, not just curiosity?

- Have I considered unintended impacts on others?

Group Work:

- Have I clearly explained the ritual and gotten active consent?

- Am I giving credit for borrowed rituals or symbols?

- Am I open to questions and feedback?

- Have I checked my own motivations?

Cross-Cultural Exploration:

- Did I research cultural context and meaning?

- Does the practice require permission or training?

- Am I supporting living practitioners or communities?

- Am I prepared to step back if needed?

Keep this checklist nearby for easy access. Before starting any new or unfamiliar practice, review each question on the list and answer honestly. Use the checklist as a decision-making tool: read it before you begin a ritual or group activity, and revisit it whenever you feel unsure about your choices. Print it out or save it to your phone for quick reference, so you remember to use it whenever guidance is needed.

Building trust starts with ethics. When you act in line with your values, you prevent harm and foster genuine connection. For example, researching a ritual's origin helped me choose to avoid closed practices. Sometimes, it's best to say no. Ethics keeps your path authentic and connects you with others in lasting ways.

Navigating Online and Offline Magical Communities Safely

Magical communities take many forms, like traditional forums, Discord servers, local moon circles, and special social media groups. You'll find everything from chaos magic to folk traditions. Local gatherings give you a face-to-face connection, but most community-building now happens online. Some groups are open and welcoming, while others are closed or secret and may require vetting or following certain traditions for safety or privacy. Open groups are usually easier to join, while closed ones can offer more trust or closeness.

When considering a new group, observe how members interact. Healthy spaces value openness, clear communication, and respect. Look for discussion, diversity, and clear boundaries. Be alert to signs of secrecy, manipulation, pressure to conform, or "one true way" thinking. If you notice coercive behaviors or exclusion, consider stepping back to protect your safety and uphold ethical standards.

Before joining a group, recognize how leaders' transparency and openness can help you feel confident and respected. Research the group or leader to understand their approach and values, which builds trust and reassurance.

If a group feels wrong, bad energy, pressure, or troubling stories, trust your instincts. You can always leave with a simple, polite message. If concerned about retaliation or harassment, block or mute members for safety.

Protect your online identity to feel safe and in control. Use pseudonyms, adjust privacy settings, and share personal details only with trusted people to foster confidence and security.

Be alert to doxxing, where your private information is exposed. Share a little about family, work, or routine. Use private profiles to restrict access. For sensitive talks, use encrypted apps or invite-only forums for security.

A community doesn't have to be big to matter. If you're new, private, or live in a rural area, it can feel lonely, but you can take action now by reaching out to one trusted friend or starting a discussion group around a favorite book. Be proactive: reading together builds trust without requiring anyone to share their full magical background. Seek out moderated online spaces with active admins and anti-harassment rules for safer, more structured connections. Join online workshops or virtual rituals to connect without risking your privacy.

Remember that quality over quantity matters. Form bonds with a few trusted individuals or small groups to create a sense of genuine support and belonging, even from a distance.

Magical groups are like any other gatherings; harmony isn't always guaranteed. Stay curious, but put your well-being and boundaries first. Trust both your instincts and your judgment when choosing where to invest your energy.

Sharing, Teaching, and Learning with Respectful Exchanges and Boundaries

Sharing or teaching magical knowledge carries new responsibilities. Your words can impact others. When passing on expertise, your care, context, and boundaries are as important as the information itself.

There's a key difference between sharing open-source wisdom (such as foundational practices, public folklore, or personal rituals) and passing along practices from closed or initiatory traditions. Open-source material is for everyone and is open to adaptation and reinterpretation. Closed or initiatory teachings, however, are private for legitimate reasons, such as safety, respect, lineage, or cultural survival. When uncertain, ask yourself: Is this mine to share? If not, it's perfectly okay to say so and point others to trusted resources.

Citing your sources is essential. If you learned something from a teacher, book, or online creator, say so. Giving credit not only shows respect but also helps others trace teachings back to their roots. It's tempting to tweak a ritual and call it your own, but honoring the source adds integrity and depth to what you share. Ultimately, everyone benefits when sources are acknowledged.

When you teach, mentor, or share, take responsibility for the impact of your words. Always seek consent, use your personal experience to frame advice, and make confidentiality explicit. Proactively set respectful boundaries, let trust, care, and consent guide every exchange you have.

Commit to upholding these practices each time you guide or support others.

Even as an "expert," practice humility. No one knows everything, regardless of experience. It's powerful to admit when you don't have an answer or are still learning. If asked to teach something outside your scope, especially from a tradition you admire but don't belong to, be honest: "That's not my practice to share, but I can point you to those who hold that knowledge." This isn't gatekeeping; it's respect for healthy boundaries.

Knowing when to share and when to hold back can be difficult. You may feel pressure, internal or external, to reveal everything you know. Practice discernment. Certain spells or rituals remain private for good reasons: they're based on oaths, are confidential, or are too personal for public sharing. Respecting this protects your practice and honors those who came before. If you ever feel exposed after sharing, listen to that discomfort; it usually signals a need to pull back.

When asked for more than you can ethically give, use scripts to set boundaries while staying open. You might say, "I'd love to share my experience, but this isn't universal advice," or, if pressed for closed knowledge, "This isn't mine to teach directly; here are some resources to learn more from insiders." Such responses maintain connection without overstepping.

Reflection deepens wisdom in these exchanges. Journal about what ethical teaching means to you, or after a complex interaction, note what worked and what you might shift next time. One teacher I knew refused to publish group rituals online, even under pressure from students. She explained her reasons and offered alternative learning paths. Her boundaries didn't exclude; they modeled care for both the tradition and her own well-being.

Not every exchange is perfect; sometimes you'll wish you had said less or more. That's natural when learning in a community. When in doubt, check in with yourself and the other person: "Was consent clear? Was the exchange mutual? Did everyone feel respected?" Asking these questions helps ensure sharing strengthens connections without crossing into territory that isn't yours.

Troubleshooting Ethical Dilemmas When Rituals Meet the Real World

Studying ethics and following checklists is one thing; truly testing your values happens when your magical practice meets daily life. Suddenly, it's not just you; other people, their boundaries, and potential consequences come into play as well. Maybe you consider performing a ritual for someone without their asking, or you're tempted to cast a discreet spell at work. Situations like a co-worker walking in while you're burning herbs can quickly become awkward and confusing.

To navigate these dilemmas, start by anchoring yourself in your core values: honesty, autonomy, kindness, and respect. Think beyond your intentions ("I want to help!") to the impact on others. Acting without someone's knowledge, even with good intentions, can cross personal boundaries, especially in close relationships or shared environments. If uncertain, pause and consider the potential effects on everyone involved, not just your end goal. What feels safe to you could be unsettling for someone else.

Workplaces and public environments add complexity. You may want to use a protective charm at your desk, but sharing a space with people of diverse beliefs requires sensitivity. Transparency isn't always feasible, or safe, in these settings. Balance your practice with respect for shared spaces and boundaries. If privacy is difficult, use subtle alternatives, like silent affirmations or visualizations, that don't affect others. Remember: your right to practice ends where someone else's comfort or consent begins.

Another challenge is conflicting worldviews. You may live with people who are skeptical or hostile toward magical practices, or with people who belong to groups with varying beliefs. Disagreements can flare up quickly, especially around cultural appropriation or differing moral codes. In heated moments, pause and listen before responding. Strive to understand their perspective, even if you strongly disagree.

Good decision-making relies on a flexible framework. Start by clarifying your intention. What do you hope to achieve? Then, realistically assess possible consequences: Who could be affected? What's the best and worst case? Are there alternatives that reduce discomfort or risk? If stuck, consult a trusted, thoughtful friend or mentor; they may spot blind spots or potential harms you've missed. When no clear answer exists, choose the path that causes the least damage and respects all involved.

Navigating Sticky Situations

If someone expresses discomfort, like a roommate who dislikes incense or a friend who is uneasy about your altar, acknowledge their feelings without defensiveness. Ask what would help them feel comfortable, and aim for compromise, whether that's changing ritual times or using scent-free methods. With group rituals, constantly revisit consent, especially if plans shift; check in with anyone who seems hesitant.

For community disputes or cultural appropriation, listen before defending yourself or your group. If possible, seek input from those within the affected culture. If you're in the wrong, be ready to change course, even if it means letting go of a cherished practice. When discussions stall, suggest a pause before making final choices.

When friends ask for magical help, clarify their expectations and beliefs first. Are they genuinely interested, or simply seeking a quick fix or something that feels uncomfortable to you? If you decline, be honest: "I care, but I'm not comfortable using magic here." If you agree to help, clearly communicate your approach and get explicit consent.

Handling Mistakes and Moving Forward

Mistakes will occur; it's part of practicing magic in everyday life. If you cross a line or make someone uncomfortable, acknowledge it without minimizing: "I'm sorry, I didn't realize how this might affect you." Let the other person respond, and ask what might help restore trust. Don't rush or force forgiveness; show through your actions that you're learning.

Ethical dilemmas can be daunting, but they often teach far more than theory ever will. Each conflict is a chance to clarify your values, not only in magic, but in becoming the kind of person you want to be in all aspects of life.

Authentic Voices, Real Journeys, Real Lessons

What truly shapes us as magical or mystical practitioners isn't flawless rituals or polished social feeds. It's the authentic, sometimes awkward, often inspiring stories from people making real choices in messy situations. Theories have their place, but genuine growth happens where confusion, hope, regret, and wisdom overlap. Here, I share lived experiences to illustrate how nuanced ethical learning unfolds in practice, not as perfect models, but as honest examples of grappling with real-life complexities.

Take M., a solitary practitioner feeling isolated in a conservative area. Online forums became vital, but many groups seemed more interested in drama than genuine connection. After witnessing heated debates about cultural borrowing, M. chose a different approach. Instead of arguing, she reached out privately to thoughtful individuals, asked questions, and listened. Over time, she built her own supportive network, where curiosity and learning from mistakes were valued. For her, community wasn't joining an ideal group but finding a few honest, kind allies.

Consider also the story of a ritual group known for inclusiveness and creativity. One year, they based a celebration on a tradition from another culture, thinking that adaptation would honor diversity. When a new member expressed discomfort and explained why this felt disrespectful, the group listened. They researched, invited feedback from people rooted in that tradition, and eventually changed their plans. The process was complicated, and some felt let down, but most agreed it deepened their understanding of respect and boundaries. Their readiness to adapt marked a crucial turn in their growth.

Burnout among teachers and mentors is common. J., a longtime workshop leader, loved teaching but felt exhausted by endless demands for more, especially requests for free advice or custom spells. When she realized she was dreading these interactions, she decided to draw more precise boundaries, say no more often, and ensure time for her rest and personal practice. While some people pushed back, most respected her honesty. The changes restored her joy in teaching, on her terms.

New practitioners also stumble, often with the best intentions. Sam was eager at his first group ritual and brought a friend without warning anyone or explaining what to expect. When the friend panicked and left mid-ritual, Sam felt terrible. The group leader had a challenging yet caring conversation with him, emphasizing the importance of obtaining consent from everyone involved. That lesson, embarrassing as it was, reshaped how Sam handled rituals, emphasizing honest communication and clear invitations.

These stories aren't neat solutions or scripts to copy. They reveal how real-life practice is layered with emotion and context, often requiring us to pause, listen, adapt, or admit mistakes. Ethical action may mean speaking up, stepping back, or apologizing. Whether you're a leader, a newcomer, or in between, these experiences show that community and integrity are built through steady, sometimes uncomfortable effort.

As you reflect on these stories, consider your own journey: a time you wish you'd acted differently or handled something well. What did you learn? How did it shape your sense of right and wrong? You might jot down these reflections: "What ethical challenge have I faced in magical or mystical practice? What did I learn?" Bring these questions to your book club or discussion group; conversation often leads to fresh insights. Or, if you're comfortable, share your story with someone you trust or in your journal. Clarity and comfort come simply from expressing your experience.

These case studies aren't about blame or chasing moral perfection. They show that being human means fumbling at times, and that's normal. What matters is how we respond: listening, learning, and moving forward with greater care.

As you finish this chapter, remember: ethics aren't fixed rules. They live in your choices, relationships, and willingness to grow. Everything here invites you to engage with magic and mysticism boldly and humbly. Next, we'll explore how to integrate these principles into lasting, evolving spiritual practices.

Chapter Ten

Advanced Practices and Lifelong Integration

Mixing Traditions Mindfully to Build Your Unique Path

It's exciting to realize your practice doesn't have to follow just one path. You might blend incense, mantras, and Tarot cards from different traditions. Today, as you create your own mix, freedom calls for research, honest reflection, and mindful listening before adding new elements to your practice.

When you blend traditions, it's essential to understand their roots and context. Ask yourself: Do I know the story behind this practice? Am I honoring its origins? Deep research, especially from people within the tradition, is essential, especially if the path is new to you. Don't use something just because it seems "magical." Mixing things without care can lead to misunderstandings and hide what's sacred or protected. Being respectful means adapting with care for context; appropriation is using material from marginalized cultures without understanding or permission.

A simplified decision flow for blending practices:

- Do you understand its cultural meaning? If not, research more.

- Is the practice open to others? If unsure, seek guidance.

- Will you credit its origins every time? If not sure, pause and reflect.

Once, I added a new chant to my ritual because I liked how it sounded. After a week, though, it felt out of place. I realized I hadn't respected its origins or checked if it fit with my other practices. So, I changed my opening to thank each tradition: "With gratitude to the teachers of Tarot, the wisdom of Buddhist breathwork, and the guardians of this land..." That small change helped my ritual feel right again.

Creating an altar for a blended path is also a way to show respect. Choose objects that represent each tradition, like a Tarot card for one, a mala for another, or a stone that connects to your ancestors. Use opening and closing rituals to honor each tradition, for example: "May this practice honor the ancestors of both lineages and support my growth with respect." These actions help keep your practice honest and grounded.

As you grow, make it a habit to check in with yourself, especially after adding something new. Every few months, ask what's working and what feels forced or out of step with your values or feelings. Write down your reactions, like excitement, discomfort, pride, or guilt, as you try new practices. If something makes you uneasy, be honest about it in your journal. Don't ignore these feelings; they often point to deeper questions about who you are, where you belong, or your sense of power.

Self-Assessment Flowchart

Should I Blend This Practice?

- Do I know its cultural roots and context?

  - Yes: Continue.

  - No: Research more.

- Is this practice open to others?

  - Yes: Continue.

  - No/Unsure: Seek guidance or choose another element.

- Will I honor and credit its source each time?

  - Yes: Integrate mindfully.

  - No: Reconsider use.

- After including it, do I feel expanded or uneasy?

  - Expanded: Proceed with reflection.

  - Uneasy: Pause; journal and explore why.

In the end, blending traditions isn't about collecting impressive rituals. It's about building a living practice that respects every origin and creates a real, grounded space for your own story.

Advanced Rituals to Expand Beyond the Basics

Once you're comfortable with foundational rituals, you can explore more intricate practices that unfold over days or weeks and demand deeper focus. These go far beyond lighting a candle and making a wish; they're layered, intentional, and unique to you. A typical advanced approach is the multi-phase ritual, often lasting an entire lunar cycle or marking major transitions. For instance, an intention might start at the new moon. Each day as the moon waxes, you perform related actions to build this intention. When the full moon arrives, you conduct a ritual to amplify your goal. As the moon wanes, you focus on releasing what's no longer needed, completing the cycle. Rites of passage, like birthdays, endings, moving, or big choices, can include steps such as writing letters to your past self, burning symbols of old habits, or deliberately stepping over a threshold. Often, these actions are spaced out over days. Connecting these steps with seasonal festivals can further deepen your sense of alignment with natural cycles.

As your ritual practice grows, advanced techniques like pathworking, invocation, and evocation can deepen your experience. Pathworking involves a guided meditation in which you move through an imagined mental landscape, meeting guides or encountering symbols to strengthen your intuition and subconscious connection. Invocation is the act of inviting a quality, archetype, or deity into your awareness, influencing your thoughts and actions. Evocation differs in that it brings energy or presence into an object or space, rather than into yourself. Each step requires focus and preparation, so always ground yourself before beginning and have a straightforward way to end the practice if you feel overwhelmed.

Group rituals offer another dimension, harnessing collective energy for shared intentions or healing. Whether meeting online or in person, each participant contributes something: a spoken poem, a candle, music. The ritual structure is similar to solitary work, but amplified by shared energy. When a group voices intentions or blessings together, the experience can be especially moving. Still, solitary rites remain powerful and personal. You might design your own self-initiation for a new life phase, or a ritual to release a former identity, like after a breakup or job change. Personalize the experience with symbols that hold meaning, like a song, water for cleansing, or a token to wear as a reminder.

Using layers of symbolism deepens rituals. To make your ritual more powerful, think about timing and setting. Astrological timing can add energy to your rite, like choosing sunrise for new beginnings or certain planetary days, such as Venus for love, or planning around retrogrades for alignment. Many people avoid moon voids to keep their intentions steady. Even the weather can add meaning, like rain for cleansing or wind for letting go. Nature is a powerful setting; performing a ritual outside, in a park, or under a favorite tree often increases your sense of connection and meaning.

Sound and movement can change your state of mind. Try adding drumming, chanting, or singing to help you focus; music connects your intention to both body and mind. You can also add movement, like swaying or walking, to make rituals feel more real. Incantations, which are spoken words with rhythm, help anchor your intent. Repeating them, whether quietly or aloud, tells your subconscious that something important is happening.

After a deep ritual, give yourself time to return slowly to everyday life. Ground yourself by eating, washing your face, or holding something solid. Journaling soon after helps you remember your thoughts before they fade. Write about what you saw, felt, or wondered. Art can also help you process your experience; try sketching symbols or scenes from your ritual. Sometimes, new insights will come to you days later.

Support is essential in advanced practice. Trusted friends can help you process group rituals, and a mentor or therapist can offer clarity if strong emotions come up. If you're working alone and feel overwhelmed, take a break and reach out to someone. Having someone who understands or can listen makes transformation safer and more sustainable.

Most of all, stay curious and open to change. Some of the most powerful rituals are simple and heartfelt, while others need careful planning. Your needs and preferences will change over time, and that's normal. Being flexible is what keeps your ritual practice meaningful and alive.

Divination as Dialogue with Tarot, Runes, and Beyond for Personal Guidance

Divination isn't just about telling the future. It's an ongoing conversation with your intuition, inner wisdom, and the unknown. When you use tools like Tarot cards or runes, you're not just trying to "see the future"—you're starting a process that can help you understand your present. The real value lies in the questions you ask and in how you interpret the answers. Don't treat divination as a vending machine for answers; use it to explore your curiosity, reflect on your mood, and spark creativity when things feel uncertain. Honest questions about your feelings, decisions, or next steps invite guidance that helps you sort out your priorities and find clarity. Sometimes the cards or symbols you draw might surprise or confuse you. When that happens, pause and ask, "What's really being shown to me right now?" Struggling with uncertainty can yield more insight than simply seeking clear answers.

Choosing your tools is a personal journey, like finding a friend or a favorite song. Pay attention to what feels right for you. Tarot decks use images and stories, which are great if you like visuals; each card represents classic archetypes and stories. Runes are hands-on and give direct symbolic meaning. The I Ching offers deep, poetic wisdom for those who enjoy complexity. Lenormand decks give quick, practical readings, while pendulums are good if you trust movement and intuition. Bibliomancy, or randomly opening books, is perfect if you love words and surprises. There's no wrong tool; use what interests you. If you don't want to buy special items, you can improvise with coins, pages from your journal, or even song lyrics.

Once you feel comfortable, try moving from simple drawings to more complex layouts. Advanced Tarot spreads, for example, can show your goals, hidden influences, and practical advice all at once, giving you a fuller picture of any issue. With runes, a three-stone cast (past, present, emerging) helps you notice patterns and changes over time. Complex spreads aren't just about using more cards; they encourage deeper questions and let connections appear naturally. Mix traditional meanings with your own intuition and life experience. When a symbol stands out, like the Tower or Hagalaz, don't rush to look it up online. Trust your first impression as part of the message.

Divination requires self-awareness and respect, not just curiosity. It's easy to read whenever you feel anxious, or to keep asking the same question, hoping for a different answer. Try to avoid this. Set honest limits on your sessions and give yourself time between readings so your insights can settle. If a spread looks "bad" or unsettling, see it as an opportunity for greater self-awareness. These moments often point to growth or truths you've overlooked. Instead of fearing certain cards or symbols, ask yourself, "What might I need to face or understand here?" This approach helps you build resilience and makes divination more useful.

Journaling after readings makes the process much richer. Write down not only what came up, but also the deeper question that might be behind your reading. Sometimes, what we ask on the surface hides bigger themes like self-worth, trust, or freedom. Use your journal as a safe space to reflect, write your interpretations, note your feelings, and capture any sudden insights.

Reading for others comes with extra responsibility. Always ask for permission before doing a reading, and never force a reading on someone who isn't ready. When you read for friends or groups, make it clear that your role is to offer perspective, not to decide their fate. Keep what comes up in a reading private. Encourage others to see divination as a conversation and invite honest discussion about what feels true and what doesn't, rather than expecting everyone to agree politely.

In the end, divination becomes a living relationship. It's a way to check in with yourself and your world when life feels complicated. The more you treat it as a conversation instead of just looking for fixed answers, the more meaningful and helpful it will be.

Resource for Curated Reading, Teachers, and Community Connections

Finding the right teacher or mentor can feel like searching for a rare book in a chaotic shop. Many claim wisdom, but not all offer the depth and genuine care you deserve. Before committing to any class, mentorship, or retreat, trust your instincts: do you feel respected and seen? Is the teacher open about their background, lineage, and influences? A trustworthy mentor credits their sources, openly discusses their journey, and welcomes questions. Good teachers admit what they don't know, respond honestly, and foster your curiosity. Ask about their experience: How long have they practiced? Who did they study with? How do they handle ethics and boundaries? Quality teachers encourage dialogue and support you in developing your own approach, rather than insisting you copy theirs. Compatibility is as important as credentials; if you frequently feel confused, dismissed, or shamed, it's wise to move on.

Before investing your time or money, clarify logistics: What are the actual learning goals? Is there individual feedback, or is it strictly lecture-based? Are there prerequisites or important expectations? How is your privacy protected? Are your questions and struggles kept confidential? Be cautious with teachers who aggressively market products, have vague agreements, or request large sums up front. Warning signs include claims of exclusive, secret knowledge, discouraging the use of outside resources, or blurring personal and professional boundaries. Never feel pressured to share more than you're comfortable with. Red flags include manipulation, gossip, or subtle shaming. True mentors support your growth without making themselves the center of attention.

Magic grows stronger with many different voices. The field respects both classic authors such as Dion Fortune, Starhawk, and Doreen Valiente, as well as new leaders expanding the conversation. Look for teachers who value inclusivity and try to learn from different perspectives. Modern voices often discuss identity, activism, trauma, and cultural context, topics essential to a healthy practice. Don't hesitate to reach out to authors or join their online events; many are more accessible than you might think.

Community is just as crucial as studying on your own. If you want a connection, there are many options. Major conferences and festivals, such as Pantheacon (when it's running), Mystic South, and other regional pagan gatherings, offer workshops, rituals, and chances to meet others. Online forums are different: some, like Reddit's r/witchcraft, specific Discord servers, or well-moderated Facebook groups, offer support and good information. Others might have drama or spread misinformation. Try things out before getting too involved, and notice how newcomers are treated and if moderators keep things respectful.

Smaller communities can have a greater impact than large groups. Book clubs that focus on magical texts lead to good discussions and help you put ideas into practice. Accountability partners, even just one or two friends, help you stay motivated and on track. Practice circles, whether online or in person, give you a chance to share rituals without pressure. You can learn a lot just by watching how others make their practices their own. If you can't find a group that fits, think about starting your own: pick a theme, set clear rules, and take turns leading so everyone feels included.

As your network grows, it's essential to stay organized. Make a "resource map" to keep track of your favorite books, teachers, safe communities, and inspiring contacts. This could be as simple as a notebook page with categories like "Texts," "People," "Groups," and "Events," or you could use a digital tool like a spreadsheet. Add links, helpful notes, and upcoming events. Every few months, look over your map and update it. Ask yourself what's missing, where you feel stuck, or where you want more experience. This helps you spot gaps; maybe you need more ancestor work or more hands-on practice instead of just theory.

Column Headings for a Resource Map Table

> Category
> Name
> Title
> Contact
> Link
> Notes
> Impressions
> Next Steps
> Books
> Teachers
> Groups
> Events

Think of this as a living document. Whenever you find a great book or meet an inspiring mentor, add them to your resource map. Note what works for you and what doesn't. Check in with yourself regularly: Where do you want to grow? What topics excite or intimidate you? Who can you ask for help? Update your map as your experiences and interests change.

Maintaining Inspiration and Growth Over Time

Keeping your magical practice alive and meaningful over the years can be both rewarding and challenging. After the first excitement fades, you might notice your rituals feel repetitive, or you try to do more but enjoy it less. If you ever feel tired, uninspired, or just going through the motions, you're not broken. It's a sign your spirit needs a change. Spiritual fatigue can sneak up on you, showing up as boredom, irritation, or even guilt. You might skip rituals you once loved, feel resentful about commitments, or stop caring about your tools and symbols. The answer isn't to push yourself harder. Real growth comes from learning to rest, step back, and renew yourself.

Getting rest is just as important as the celebration. Plan breaks where you step away from your usual practice to recharge. Nature is a good example; fields need time to rest before they can grow again. Take a weekend off from anything magical, or try a "ritual fast." Put away your altar and tools, turn off podcasts and books, and let yourself enjoy the quiet. Inspiration often comes back in these quiet moments when you least expect it. Sometimes, the best thing for your practice is a walk in the park or a night out with friends, not another spell or meditation.

Knowing when you've outgrown certain beliefs or routines is a valuable skill. Every year, or whenever it feels right, try doing a personal review ritual. Light a candle, open your journal, and ask yourself three questions: What am I truly grateful for this year? What am I ready to let go of? What do I want to welcome next? This isn't just about magical goals, it's about your whole self. Maybe you notice a tool doesn't feel right anymore, or an old affirmation feels forced. Letting go could mean donating books, putting away an old altar cloth, or simply thanking practices that helped you and moving on.

Feeling stuck is normal, but it doesn't have to last. When you feel stagnant, try something new to spark your creativity. Learn a new art form, like painting, dancing, or poetry, or try physical activities like yoga or hiking. Sometimes, inspiration comes from outside the magical world. Cooking a dish from another culture, visiting a museum, or volunteering in your community can help you rediscover your sense of wonder. If you want more structure, keep a "curiosity list," a page in your journal or phone, where you write down practices that interest you. When you have more energy, pick something from the list to try.

New teachers and fresh traditions can give you a new perspective. Look for workshops, podcasts, or books that are outside your usual interests. Join group projects, like creating a ritual with friends or joining an online discussion. Working with others often leads to ideas you wouldn't have on your own. Don't be afraid to travel, even if it's just a short trip to a nearby town or forest; a change of scenery can shift your energy in unexpected ways.

Patience is often overlooked, but it can change everything. You don't have to reinvent yourself every season or keep up with others. Many practitioners I know have gone through significant changes, like becoming parents, facing illness, or growing into new roles, and their magic changed with them. One friend stopped all group rituals after her first child was born, but years later found new meaning in small moments with her toddler. Another friend managed chronic illness by moving from big ceremonies to quiet meditations in bed, and found just as much depth in stillness.

Humility can open doors that pride cannot. Sometimes, the most significant changes happen slowly, a slight shift in attitude, letting go of comparing yourself to others, or being willing to try and fail without shame. Community helps with this, too. Celebrate small wins, like finishing a month of daily gratitude or getting through a hard time without giving up. Ask for support when you need it; there's nothing wrong with seeking advice or encouragement when your motivation is low.

Something to Think About

How will you nurture your magic for the next decade? Write, without editing, about what you most want to sustain, what you hope to release, and how you'll remind yourself that slow growth is still growth.

As this chapter ends, remember that magic isn't about always moving faster. It's about rhythm and renewal. Your practice will deepen when you honor both rest and action, look for inspiration outside your comfort zone, and treat yourself kindly through every change. The next chapter will show how magic can be part of all areas of life, like relationships, work, health, and creativity, helping you stay open to new possibilities every day.

Conclusion

If you're reading this, you've finished a journey that's not just about candles, symbols, or old names. It's about you, your search for meaning, your curiosity, and your willingness to try something new, even when it feels strange. I wrote this book to help you find ways to bring magic and mysticism into your daily routine. I want you to feel confident, creative, and ethical as you use these practices. You don't have to feel like you're pretending, or that you must pick between tradition and your own truth. You can have both.

Let's pause and look back at what we've covered. We began by exploring what magic and mysticism mean today. We moved past stereotypes and pop culture ideas, focusing on intention, presence, and self-trust. Looking at history, we see how different cultures have shaped what we call "magic." You learned that you don't have to be a historian to respect tradition, but having some background helps keep your practice meaningful.

From there, we rolled up our sleeves. You learned how to craft rituals with what you already have: kitchen spoons, favorite mugs, music playlists, and all. We tackled grounding, protection, and cleansing. Modern life throws a lot at us, and a little energetic hygiene never hurts. You tried adaptable rituals, some short, some long, testing what fits your schedule and spirit. We played with symbols, archetypes, and personal meaning. This helped you build a language that fits your own life, not just what's found in old books.

We explored self-reflection and shadow work. Real transformation asks us to look at our fears and uncomfortable parts, not just the moments that look good online. You discovered the power in beauty, music, and your senses, making things like altars or tea feel special. We talked openly about ethics, sharing checklists and stories from people who learned to respect boundaries and cultures, even when it was difficult. The tools, frameworks, and reflection prompts in these pages are here for you to revisit, tweak, and expand as your needs change.

So what do you take from this? You now have practical skills. They aren't just for rituals or incense, but also for noticing your intuition, thinking about your choices, and adjusting your practice to fit your life. You have ways to make your magic personal and lasting. You also have tools for practicing ethically, honoring both tradition and modern life. Most of all, you've built self-trust that will help you long after you finish this book.

Remember, magic isn't about doing it the "right" way according to others. It's about being there for yourself, trying things out, reflecting, making mistakes, laughing, and trying again. The best rituals are those that feel real to you: in your body, your home, and your own way. You choose what works. No one else gets to decide.

It's normal to have doubts, questions, or to feel awkward and unsure sometimes. That's not failure; it shows you're thinking and growing. Your questions are welcome, and your changing beliefs matter. Whether you're a skeptic, a believer, a dabbler, or somewhere in between, you belong here.

Remember the bigger picture. Magic and mysticism are about connecting to yourself, others, the world, and mystery. Practice with respect. Pay attention to where your rituals and tools come from. If you make a mistake, pause, learn, or say sorry. The world needs people who practice with honesty, humility, and care for communities and traditions.

You don't have to do this by yourself. There are communities out there: a book club, a Discord group, a local circle, or friends who understand. Share what you experience. Ask questions. Give support. Set boundaries.

Choose how and with whom you connect. Even if you practice alone, you're still part of something larger.

If you remember one thing from this book, let it be this: your magical path is yours to shape and grow. You can go back to old chapters. Change your mind. Try new things. Rest when you need to. Let this book be a touchstone, a place you can return to for ideas, help, or a reminder that you're not alone in wanting more from life.

Here's my invitation: choose one ritual, exercise, or reflection from this book and try it today. Light a candle. Write a wish. Bless your coffee. Sit and notice your breath. Write down how it felt. That's your start, or your next start. Magic is alive, and every day is a new chance to begin.

Thank you for trusting me on this journey. Thank you for letting yourself be curious, even when it felt uncomfortable. I hope you keep trusting your instincts, creativity, and unique wisdom. The magic you're looking for is inside you. You're ready to let it shine.

If this book helped you, please leave an honest review.

Thank you,

George Munson

Glossary

Glossary

Altar: A dedicated space (physical or virtual) for magical work, often adorned with candles, statues, crystals, and other magical tools, including symbols and focus.

Astral Travel: The experience of journeying outside the physical body, often during meditation or dreams.

Athame: A ritual knife, usually used to direct energy within a circle (not for physical cutting).

Banishing: The act of removing unwanted energies or influences, often through ritual or visualization.

Book of Shadows: A personal grimoire or journal of magical practices, results, and reflections.

Calling the Quarters: Invoking the powers of the four cardinal directions (and their associated elements) during ritual.

Circle Casting: Creating sacred space by energetically "drawing" a circle, a foundational step in many rituals.

Cleansing: Purifying space, tools, or oneself—often with smoke (smudging), salt, or sound.

Correspondences: The associations (like herbs, colors, planets) linked to magical outcomes ("Rosemary corresponds to remembrance and protection").

Coven: A group of practitioners, often witches, who meet regularly for rituals and study.

Divination: Techniques for seeking guidance or insight (tarot, runes, pendulums, etc.).

Familiars: Animal companions believed to aid magical work (real pets or spirit guides).

Grimoire: A personal book of spells, rituals, and magical notes—often lovingly crafted and decorated.

Grounding and Centering: Techniques for anchoring one's energy and focus, often before or after magical work.

Grounding: Techniques for reconnecting with the body or Earth after magical work (e.g., "I grounded with hematite after the ritual").

High Magic / Low Magic: "High" refers to ceremonial, philosophical traditions (like Hermeticism); "low" to folk or practical magic (like kitchen witchery).

Mundane: Refers to ordinary, non-magical reality or tasks ("Back to the mundane world after ritual").

Pathworking: Guided visualization or meditation journeys used to access inner wisdom or magical insight.

Shadow Self: The hidden or unacknowledged parts of the psyche.

Shadow Work: Exploring and integrating one's unconscious or repressed aspects through journaling, meditation, or therapy.

Sigil: A symbol created for a specific magical purpose, charged with intent and often activated through ritual.

Wheel of the Year: The annual cycle of pagan festivals, including Sabbats like Samhain, Beltane, and Lammas.

References

7 Space-Saving altar designs that won't alter your home's aesthetic! (n.d.). Qanvast. https://qanvast.com/sg/articles/7-space-saving-altar-designs-that-wont-alter-your-homes-aesthetic-2984

Billock, J. (2020, September 3). Confronting appropriation in Witchcraft. *KitchenWitch*. https://kitchenwitch.substack.com/p/confronting-appropriation-in-witchcraft

Buggy, P. (2017, July 13). *How to cultivate Beginner's mind for a fresh perspective | Mindful Ambition*. Mindful Ambition. https://mindfulambition.net/beginners-mind/

Circle casting and sacred space. (n.d.). https://www.controverscial.com/Circle%20Casting%20and%20Sacred%20Space.htm

Eileen, S. (2022, October 27). *Unconventional tools and altar supplies*. By Sidney Eileen. https://sidneyeileen.com/2019/11/19/unconventional-tools-and-altar-supplies/

Farley, H. (2016). Religion, the Occult, and the Paranormal: Ideas, practices and groups. *Canterbury-nz*. https://www.academia.edu/22465171/Religion_the_Occult_and_the_Paranormal_Ideas_practices_and_groups

Ferris, P. (2025, November 11). *How to Cast a Spell: A beginner's guide to magic rituals*. wikiHow. https://www.wikihow.com/Cast-a-Spell

Grandma. (2025, January 22). A Witch's Guide to Moon Magick » Grandma's Grimoire. *Grandmas Grimoire*. https://grandmasgrimoire.com/a-witchs-guide-to-moon-magick/

Gyrus. (2016, December 5). *Chaos and Beyond - Dreamflesh*. Dreamflesh. https://dreamflesh.com/interview/phil-hine/

Jeffrey, S. (2025, December 24). *A Beginner's Guide to Jungian Shadow Work: How to Integrate Your Dark Side*. CEOsage. https://scottjeffrey.com/shadow-work/

Kristen. (2021, July 14). *Alternatives to sage for cleansing - Good Witch kitchen*. https://www.goodwitchkitchen.net/cleansing-without-sage/

Larsen, C., & Larsen, C. (2020, July 25). *Daily Witchcraft: 10 simple Ways to Practice Magic everyday*. Mage by Moonlight. https://magebymoonlight.com/daily-witchcraft-practice-magic-every day/

Magic, & Magic. (2025, August 8). *Sneaky Spells: Low-Key Magick you can do in Public | Witches Lore*. Witcheslore. https://witcheslore.com/bookofshadows/rituals-spell-casting/sneaky -spells-low-key-magick-you-can-do-in-public/

Mentoring Aspiring Graduate students and building an Inclusive Community (MAGIC). (2025, December 18). *Home*. Mentoring Aspiring Graduate Students and Building an Inclusive Community (MAGIC). https://magic.initiative.uconn.edu/

Meyer, F. (2024, December 9). *Spiritual journaling: How to keep a spiritual journal, and 46 spiritual journal prompts*. Writers.com. https://writers.com/spiritual-journaling-how-to-keep-a-spiritual-jour nal-and-spiritual-journal-prompts

Raypole, C. (2025, February 20). *30 Grounding techniques to quiet distressing thoughts*. Healthline. https://www.healthline.com/health/grounding-techniques

Saguil, A., & Phelps, K. (2012, September 15). *The spiritual assessment*. AAFP. https://www.aafp.org/pubs/afp/issues/2012/0915/p546.html

Vernon, J. (2025, May 1). *Using magical doors for skrying on the tree of life*. Joy Vernon Astrology * Tarot * Reiki. https://joyvernon.com/using-magical-doors-for-skrying-on-the-tree-of-life/

Whisperer, F. (2026, January 13). Ethical Foraging and Sustainable Green Witchcraft - 21 ways to make a difference - A Green Witch. *A Green Witch*. https://agreenwitch.com/sustainable-green-witchcraft/